PENGUIN BOOKS

How To Invest Your Money & Profit From Inflation

Morton Shulman was born and educated in Toronto and still carries on the general practice of medicine he established at the time he married in 1950.

Shulman has always been an outspoken, and often controversial, man in the forefront. "He was nationally known as chief coroner for Toronto and was later very popularly elected to two terms in the Ontario Legislature. Presently, he is syndicated columnist for *The Toronto Sun* and host of the weekly television show, "The Shulman File".

Along the way, he has travelled and lectured extensively and has had six books published.

How to Invest
Your Money
& Profit from
INFLATION

Morton Shulman

How to Invest Your Money & Profit from INFLATION

Penguin Books

Penguin Books Ltd, Harmondsworth, Middlesex, England
Penguin Books, 625 Madison Avenue, New York, New York 10022, U.S.A.
Penguin Books Australia Ltd, Ringwood, Victoria, Australia
Penguin Books Canada Ltd, 2801 John Street, Markham, Ontario, Canada L3R 1B4
Penguin Books (N.Z.) Ltd, 182 – 190 Wairau Road, Auckland 10, New Zealand

—

First published in Canada by Hurtig Publishers 1979
Second edition published in Canada 1980
Published in Penguin Books 1980

—

Copyright © Morton Shulman 1980
All rights reserved

—

Cover design by Capon &
Associates Ltd.

—

Back Cover Photograph
Courtesy of CITY T.V. and Bert Brown

—

Manufactured in Canada by Webcom Limited

Contents

Back So Soon?

It is only one year since I completed the first edition of *How to Invest Your Money & Profit from Inflation*, but when the book came out in May of 1979 even I did not dream that inflation would progress quite this rapidly. The first edition sold over 50,000 copies and was first on the best-seller list in Canada for over six months last year. My advice has proven to be almost 100% accurate, which is personally very gratifying, but today in 1980 the book is already dated and my publisher has asked for a new, updated and revised edition.

To illustrate just how much change has occurred in one year, here are the suggestions for profitable investments that were included in the introduction to the first edition:

For $50, you can buy a 200-year-old painting.
For $57.84, you can buy a 1927 Lindbergh stamp.
For $120, you can buy a case of 1970 Palmer.
For $250, you can buy one Krugerrand.
For $400, you can buy 100 Welkom.

For $500, you can buy 1,000 German marks.

For $700, you can buy 100 Southvaal.

For $1,000, you can buy a Samurai Bond.

For $1,000, you can buy one share in a commodity fund.

For $1,000, you can buy a unit in an offshore fund.

For $3,000, you can sell one GNMA.

For $10,000, you can open a commodity account.

For $100,000, you can buy one share in an oil drilling fund.

By January of 1980 the 1977 Lindbergh had doubled, the Welkom and Southvaal had gone up by 200%, the Krugerrand had gone up by 150%, the Palmer by 400% and the $3,000 put into a GNMA was worth anywhere from $20,000 to $300,000 depending on the method used. The commodity market had soared and only the German marks and the Samurai Bonds had not yet shown profits.

I am mighty proud of my forecasting record and thankful to all of you who have written to tell me of the profits you have made by following my advice. The gold boom has certainly been a boon to my readers.

The world in 1980 will continue to experience a redistribution of wealth that is greater than anything since the French Revolution. After fifty years of growing affluence, the ordinary citizen is now seeing a slippage in his standard of living. Every year he makes more money, but finds that it buys fewer goods. "Solid" investments like government bonds yield less than the loss in their true value due to inflation. The majority of the population is getting a little poorer every year. But this general attrition in buying ability does not affect everyone. A few people are keeping up with inflation and a handful are jumping far ahead of it.

This second edition of *How to Invest Your Money & Profit from Inflation* remains an explanation of methods whereby the investor with moderate resources can learn techniques that will preserve capital and living standards in the inflationary spiral that in recent years has been so rapid.

The Old Virtues Are Dead

In 1979 we saw the greatest rise in interest rates in the history of Canada accompanied by a collapse in the bond market, a further deterioration in the stock market and an increasing awakening on the part of the public that something is seriously wrong with our economy.

This letter from a man in Pittsburgh is typical of hundreds that I have received in the past year:

Dear Dr. Shulman:

I saw you on the Lou Gordon Show five years ago telling listeners to buy the biggest most expensive house they could afford with the largest mortgage on it on which they could meet the payments, and at the time both my wife and I decided you were a little "off". At just about the same time we bought U.S. treasury notes paying 8% which are coming due next month. We now realize it was us who were off as we have lost horribly in buying power. We will never buy government bonds again but don't know what we should buy. What is your advice?

My advice was contained in the first edition of this book, and in 1980 I can say that the old virtues really are dead.

I grew up on them too. My father was a life insurance salesman and the company for which he worked distributed a pamphlet called *Save for a Rainy Day*. Dad tried to instill the precepts from that little booklet in our home:

- Don't buy anything you can't afford.
- Savings are essential before beginning any investment program.
- Life insurance is the best form of investment.
- Don't borrow money.
- Don't speculate, but if you must then buy a mortgage.
- Don't buy real estate. It's better to rent.
- Government bonds are the safest place to put your money.

That philosophy made sense in the thirties but it has proven a trap for so many people who grew up in those depressed days. Anyone following my father's advice today would be headed straight towards economic disaster because of inflation.

It is very hard to accept that all the old "safe" investments, the type that bankers suggested for widows and orphans and all those who couldn't afford to lose their money, are now certain to produce losses. Not losses in terms of number of dollars, but losses where it *really* counts: in *buying power*. It is not easy to stop thinking in terms of the number of dollars you earn even though that is no longer a constant concept. When I was a young doctor, I earned $20,000 a year and thought I was rich. Now I earn many times that and have no greater buying power with my salary alone than I had twenty years ago. The problem is that few wage earners can keep up with inflation by increases in salary.

As I write this chapter in 1980, the current inflation rate is 11% per annum. An increase in my salary of 11% will not hold me even because I must pay the full 11% increase in prices, but I do not receive the full 11% increase in salary. The reason of course is income tax. If you are in the 50% income bracket, you must get a 22% raise just to stay even during inflation.

How does this situation affect traditional investments?

Government Bonds

What could be safer than a loan to the government of your country backed by the full resources of the nation's treasury? Let us consider just such an investment, one of the most common made in North America today. Suppose that in 1979 you had taken $1,000 and bought a government savings bond paying 10% interest. Today your bond is still worth $1,000 and to boot you have received $100 interest. But the $1,100 you have today will not buy as much as your original $1,000 would have bought one year ago. And of course in addition you must pay tax to the government on your $100 "profit".

What has happened is that in this "safe" investment you have taken a *real* loss. It is all part of a huge con. Governments still issue such bonds, and banks, brokers and trust companies conspire to sell them in the name of safety and good return on capital — neither of which the investor in bonds receives. After a decade of rapid inflation, I would have thought that the public would have awakened to this fact, but they have not. Most investors still fall for the same fraud in which they have been robbed steadily and repeatedly by our governments.

And what of the foolish person who buys a government bond and keeps it ten years till maturity? At today's rate of accelerating inflation, the relatively solid $1,000 you invest today which now will buy a motorcycle will probably not even purchase a bicycle in ten years.

And don't be as foolish as the reporter from the *Burlington Gazette* who began an interview with me on November 24, 1979 by saying, "My friends think you are wrong. Twelve per cent Canada Savings Bonds are a good investment. That's a good return and your talk of loss of buying power is purely theoretical." That reporter was interested in how much money he had saved and not in what it could buy! If you are turned on by the size of your bank account you can really fool yourself, but the only thing that matters is *can you buy more or fewer goods* today with that money than you could last year? Most people cannot as their real earnings and savings are shrinking. The purpose of this book is to show you how to stop that shrinkage.

Don't buy government bonds!

Corporation Bonds

Corporation bonds are not really different from government bonds. The only variation is that in this case you are loaning your money to a corporation rather than to a government. The corporation usually pays about 1 or 2% more interest because of the possible danger of the company going broke. But here again there is no way that the interest paid will keep up with the rate of inflation.*

Don't buy corporation bonds!

*Convertible bonds are a different situation. I'll discuss these later.

Life Insurance

Investment in life insurance is an even worse place to put money than bonds. Even in stable times, buying expensive insurance is a losing proposition because one must outlive the insurance in order to get back the savings. In inflationary times, it becomes a hopeless trap.

Term insurance, for protection only, may cost $5 for $1,000 worth of insurance for one year. Insurance combined with a savings plan may cost $35 for one year with the extra $30 plus interest to be returned in twenty years. With today's inflation, those savings will be worthless in twenty years. I find it amazing that millions of these savings plan policies are sold every year, in spite of the fact that all purchasers will lose their entire savings. In 1966 as inflation was barely underway, I wrote an essay on life insurance which is even more true today. Then the only riposte of the insurance companies was that savings insurance forced those persons to save who otherwise would never do it. Perhaps that was true then. Today they should be encouraged *not* to save.

Don't buy life or savings plan insurance!

Mortgages

The purchaser of a mortgage is making exactly the same mistake as the purchaser of a bond, except that instead of loaning his money to a government or a corporation, he is loaning it to an individual and the security is a house instead of a government's treasury or a company's assets. Mortgages usually run for five or ten years and the interest rate depends on the risk. It has all the disadvantages of a bond plus the added problem of not being able to liquidate for many years. In today's financial climate, mortgages are sure to produce losses in buying power.

And don't be misled by this past year's surge in interest rates. On January 1, 1980 the prime rate was 15% and the rates for first mortgages ranged between 13 and 14%. To someone used to 6% mortgages this is pretty seductive, but don't be fooled. Five years ago 10% mortgages appeared equally attractive yet those persons buying such mortgages ended up losing in terms of real buying power. *Interest rates will continue to rise to keep up with the inflation rate* and I can foresee 25% first mortgages in this decade. Don't tie your money up in a mortgage because as inflation progresses you will be left behind.

Don't buy mortgages!

Bad Investment Advice

One of the reasons so many people hold poor investments is the vast quantity of bad advice given so freely. Once a year on my television show I do a program on investing and after every show I walk away in amazement at what "the experts" had to say. In September 1978 the four guests included two investment advisors, the associate editor of *Fortune* magazine and the head of a stock exchange. This group recommended to widows the purchase of government bonds then yielding 9%! We argued violently on air but their final line was "widows want security." Well, any widow following that terrible advice has drawn a total of $135 interest on every $1,000 invested in the eighteen months that followed the show while simultaneously suffering an inflationary loss of 15% in real buying power. To boot she has probably payed some $50 in income tax on her $135 "profit". So today she has $1,085 in 1980 funds which will buy some 15% fewer goods than she could have bought before her investment in 1978 with the original $1,000.

In November 1979 we repeated the television investment program, but this time the guests included gold bug and best-selling author Howard Ruff, a representative of the Canadian Small Business Association, a highly successful stock advisor and my own commodity broker — a man who has made millions of dollars for his clients.

The stock advisor confided that he based many of his recommendations on the status of storms on the sun, the small business expert said that the place to make big money was in donut franchises, and he was so positive and encouraging that the television station received some four hundred calls asking how to contact the man. Unfortunately we didn't learn until two weeks after the show that the small business expert was personally selling donut franchises. But the real shocker was that the commodity broker and Howard Ruff both argued that gold at its then $380 was too high and should be sold. Ruff said that he was advising his clients to sell and that he was personally short. Within four weeks both had been proven spectacularly wrong and any amateur following their advice had been burned. Three days after the program my broker called me to say, "Morty, I think you are right — Ruff and I were wrong and I'm reversing myself and buying back my gold." He is nimble and quick and was able to do this, but most investors could not so easily reverse themselves.

I hope that those of you who read this book will profit from it by not attempting to catch short-term fluctuations — I guarantee you *won't* be successful at that, but you will be if you follow the rule that during inflation one must ignore short-term trends and stay with things like gold that retain their value regardless of how much paper money the government prints. One must also learn that the self-labelled gurus are all too often more successful at selling their advice than they are in their own businesses.

And bad advice can be found in the most unlikely

places. I am a contributing editor to a company that sells a course on investing to the public. In the fall of 1978, the general manager of the company requested that I write a lesson on inflation for their clients and he gave me an outline to follow which began: "When to use bonds and other fixed-income investments". I was quite surprised, but when I suggested to him that there was no place for this type of investment during an inflation, he replied, "Morty I know you're right, but there are some people who just can't sleep if their money is in gold or real estate or stocks or anything that fluctuates. Their psyche requires the security of a bond and it's our job to advise them as best we can. You have to give this older type investor someplace to put his money where he feels that he has safety of capital."

It is true that all of the traditional books on investment advice start off by saying that the three qualities to look for in any investment are in order of importance:

(1) safety of capital;
(2) yield;
(3) possibility of capital appreciation.

The hardest possible thing for an investor to accept is that there is no longer *any investment* that will guarantee safety of capital and the traditional ways in which such safety was sought — bonds, life insurance or mortgages — not only fail to give safety, they guarantee a loss of true capital. In today's economic climate there are no risk-free investments.

Worse, there is no way of getting a yield since there is no investment available in North America today which gives any yield at all. It is true that stocks and bonds give dividends and pay interest ranging from 2 to 15% per year but in no single case does this yield exceed the inflation rate. Thus, investing in a bond paying 10% with the inflation rate at 12% shows not only no true yield, but a real loss of 2% at the end of the year. In fact, the loss is even greater than this since part of the existing "interest" actually goes to taxes.

The result of our inflation is that neither safety of capital or yield are possible and we must instead look to the third factor, capital appreciation, because it is our only hope of keeping up. Those foolish persons who say that they only "sleep well" when their money is in the bank or in government bonds are going to end up losing a lot more than sleep before 1983 arrives.

A Little Inflation History

Our inflation began with Franklin D. Roosevelt and his brilliant economic advisor Maynard Keynes. In 1932, the United States was in the midst of a terrible depression. Millions were unemployed and bankruptcies were dragging down company after company. The stores were full of goods, but no one had money to buy them. Production was grinding to a halt, resulting in even more unemployment. It was the ultimate vicious circle.

Following Keynes' advice, Roosevelt pumped paper money which for the first time in U.S. history was not backed by gold into circulation. In fact, the U.S. greenbacks were simply IOUs. The American president set up artificial work programs like the National Recovery Administration which put the unemployed to work clearing forests, paving roads, or even painting pictures, and paid them with paper money which they in turn used to buy goods. In time, this produced a demand which set the factories to work again. The factories hired men to produce goods and so the depression cycle was broken.

It worked exactly as Keynes had predicted and gradually over the next seven years, prosperity returned to the United States and the world. The dark cloud overhanging this prosperity was the rapidly increasing amount of U.S. paper money circulating with no set value behind it. Its worth depended only upon the value the world believed was behind each dollar and every year there were more dollars. (Exactly the same thing happened to Canadian currency twenty years later.)

Aware of this problem, Keynes suggested that when good times returned the Government should use its increased revenues to retire the extra paper money printed during the depression. But this turned out to be the great flaw in the plan, for it became impossible to cut back on government spending. In 1941, just at the point when the attempt to cut expenses should have been made, the United States plunged into war, and after the war, the American Federal Government instituted a whole series of welfare schemes in order to prevent recession and voter displeasure. These ranged all the way from farm support programs to outright welfare, from food subsidies to cash grants to the arts. The net result of this was to push the federal deficit higher each successive year.

Clever economists recognized the financial trap, but politicians found it impossible to cut back. In a democracy, every election is a competition for votes and that competition is invariably won by the person or the party that promises (and sometimes delivers) the most to the largest number of people. The electorate is basically selfish. They will vote for lowering taxes and increasing benefits. They will never and have never voted for increasing taxes or cutting back on services.

For two decades, the results of this blitz of paper were quite pleasant. Social services expanded manifold, wages rose, and every year politicians were able to give the people more and more presents without increasing taxes. Of course, there was some inflation, but as late as 1966, it was running at only 3% annually in the United States and at that rate it didn't hurt anyone. Well almost no one: pensioners on very limited incomes did feel the pinch, but they didn't matter too much. They were old enough to die off before they got badly hurt and more important, they were not organized politically and so they were ignored by politicians of all parties.

In addition, until 1969 the United States shielded itself from most of the inflation by exporting it. From 1945 on, the United States Government printed vast quantities of paper money which were shipped abroad in return for French wine, German cars, Italian motorcycles and Japanese television sets. This process came a cropper in 1969 when the overseas world suddenly realized they were awash in U.S. green. That was the year much of the money came home. The French bought U.S. gold, the Russians bought wheat, and the Japanese arrived with suitcases of money and travelled across North America buying up impressionist art. This sudden influx of paper money into the U.S. economy gave inflation a big impetus. As prices began to rise, unions demanded higher wages, and various pressure groups pushed for more welfare for the poor. Neither American political party was able to withstand the welfare pressure and even so-called conservatives joined in the rush to further damage the economy by printing more money "to help the disadvantaged".

Politicians pay lip service to restricting the money supply, but no one ever takes this very seriously. In 1969, inflation in Canada had reached 4%. The leaders of the two opposition parties, David Lewis and Robert Stanfield, were campaigning across Canada, inveighing against our easy money policies. Prime Minister Trudeau noted the increasing newspaper coverage and announced in a major speech that inflation had to be tackled and that the government was therefore raising interest rates and restricting the money supply. The inevitable followed and as money became more expensive to borrow, companies restricted expansion, unemployment began to grow (to 5% of the work force), and mortgages on homes became more expensive.

The same two opposition leaders now began giving speeches decrying the results of the tight money policy and warning that Trudeau's policies were certain to produce a depression. The newspapers followed with huge stories and warning editorials, and after ninety days the pressure on Trudeau from his backbenchers became so intense that he gave in and completely reversed his monetary policies. He made the best of the situation by announcing that "inflation has been beaten" and therefore tight money was no longer necessary.

As we entered the 1970s, the inflation rate climbed above 5% and now both the U.S. and Canadian governments experimented with price and wage controls even though dozens of other nations in similar circumstances had tried that route and had failed.

The reason for the failure of price controls is obvious. To take a simple example, suppose you are a manufacturer of candy bars which you sell for 15¢ and the government passes a law saying you can't sell them for more than 15¢. All might go well for a brief period until you discover that one of the ingredients of your candy, cocoa which must be imported, has jumped in price to the extent that you can no longer manufacture your bars and make a profit. As you stop producing a shortage of candy bars follows. And the same situation applies to every manufactured commodity.

26

Price control invariably leads to shortages because no nation is self-sufficient and inflation is world-wide. Shortages lead to black markets, for there is always someone prepared to take the risks and fill the demand for a price.

It doesn't matter how severe are the measures proposed to punish breakers of the price control laws. During World War II we had penalties sufficiently serious that black marketeers could be locked up "for the duration" and in addition to the penalties, we were able to appeal to patriotism. Despite these factors there was a flourishing black market in gasoline coupons and in tires, and apartment "key money" became the rule. Laws can't prevent black markets. They can only drive up the price.

After a brief interval, both Canada and the United States abandoned their price control systems because they didn't work. By 1978, the inflation rate had climbed to 9%. This was probably the last chance to stop the inflationary process, for once the rate becomes double digit, 10% or over, it feeds on itself. At this point, the steady rise in prices becomes obvious to every shopper, and individuals and groups attempt to protect themselves by grabbing for even higher wages. However, higher wages can never keep up with the rise of inflation and in fact the struggle to keep ahead increases the rate of the inflationary spiral.

Recently in Canada we had a Conservative government that came to power stating their determination to beat inflation. Yet the first Conservative bill involving expenditures was a plan to give a mortgage tax credit which would cost this country several billion dollars over the next five years. It is very sad, but the first rule of politics is to get elected and the second to get re-elected and either an increase in taxes or a decrease in give-aways costs votes. The trouble is that there is always an opposition party promising lower taxes and more benefits and in order to keep those fellows out of office, the politicians in office must match their promises and therefore print more money.

The inevitable result is higher and higher prices and an ever lower value for our currency. Don't look to *any* politician or political party to reverse the process — this country is headed towards a terrible economic decline which will lower the standard of living of 99% of Canadians. But, I believe that each of us has a duty to protect to the best of our ability the buying power of our personal savings and the living standards of our families. It is surprisingly easy to do so.

Analysing a Classic Inflation: Germany 1914 to 1923

Most of the bad financial advice given today is not a result of fraud but rather of ignorance — ignorance of the past. Many nations have undergone inflation before us and all have followed the same basic pattern. It is surprising how few of our politicians have studied other inflations and as a result, the most amazing misconceptions abound.

In October 1977, a short-lived paper called *Magazine of Wall Street* ran adjacent articles by two self-styled experts. One said that during the great German inflation, holders of stocks suffered a relative loss of buying power while the other said exactly the opposite. It is invaluable to our understanding of our own inflationary times to analyse what actually happened in this classic inflation.

Fortunately, everything that occurred during the inflation in Germany has been recorded. Economics Professor Bresciani-Turroni worked with the Reparations Commission in Germany throughout the catastrophe. As the head of Export Control, he carefully recorded the month-by-month changes in the value of everything — stocks, bonds, mortgages, foreign exchange, etc. He published his classic study in 1932 in Italy, and it was translated into English and published by the firm of Augustus Kelley in London in 1937 under the title of *The Economics of Inflation*. I don't think any book is of greater value today.

Germany suffered inflation for similar reasons to ours: government overspending. They, too, began their waste with a war, but the culmination did not come because of welfare programs but rather because of the huge reparation payments Germany was forced to pay to the victorious nations after the war.

The inflation began on July 31, 1914, when the *Reichsbank* suspended the conversion of paper marks into gold. It ended on November 15, 1923, when the mark had sunk so low that one U.S. dollar could purchase a trillion German marks. On that day, citizens were given one new gold mark for every *trillion* old marks they held! Between those two events, the following had occurred.

For the first five years, inflation went relatively slowly with the amount of money in circulation quadrupling, the cost of living doubling and the price of gold and the U.S. dollar rising by only 50%. Then in the sixth year, gold and the dollar soared, more than doubling in the one year, while the cost of living and the money in circulation rose by another 50%. From 1919 to 1920, there occurred a characteristic common to all inflation: a massive rush to buy gold and foreign exchange. Gold went up 1,500% in the one year while the cost of imported goods rose by 1,900%. In the final phases of inflation from 1922 to 1923, imported goods and gold rose by 22,000%, domestic goods rose by 18,000% and food by 14,000%.

According to Bresciani-Turroni, the sudden collapse of the mark was due to psychological influences — a lack of confidence in the future of Germany and a desire to avoid the heavy taxes with which the Government belatedly hoped to balance its budget. It is significant to Canada and the United States that in February, 1923, Germany announced various measures to support the foreign exchange value of the mark (including making illegal the holding of gold and foreign currency), but at the same time the Government continued the printing of paper money and deficit financing. The law was almost totally ignored. In an effort to support the mark, the *Reichsbank* made a daily sale of 20 million gold marks by auction, the only result being that the gold was gone and the mark continued to sink.

The German Government was reluctant to raise interest rates for fear that this would cause a further rise in prices and unemployment. Instead they tried to ration credit, only the "more deserving firms" being given this honour. This resulted in tremendous enrichment of these few lucky companies. At the end, this policy had to be discontinued and interest rates rose finally to 30% per day.

One odd offshoot of the inflation was that at first, prices were going up faster than the exchange rate. It became profitable for Germans to travel to other countries, buy goods there, and resell them in Germany. This in turn further depressed the value of the mark. As time went on, the mark gradually ceased to be a "store of value" and savings more and more were converted into gold or foreign currency.

As the mark began to fall rapidly, unemployment fell with it and by the summer of 1922, unemployment practically disappeared. With the depreciation of the mark, foreign and home demand for goods grew. Foreigners wanted to profit by the greater purchasing power of their money in Germany and Germans were anxious to buy hard goods to get rid of their depreciating paper money. If

North America follows the same scenario, unemployment should be down considerably in 1980 from 1979.

From 1919 to 1923, there was a redistribution of wealth in Germany with a few entrepeneurs becoming tremendously rich. Because of rent control, real rents fell to almost zero, allowing employers to reduce nominal wages accordingly. Owners of rental property could no longer afford repair or taxes and many abandoned their properties.

The inflation so restricted the real income of many classes of consumers that later their demand for consumption goods fell. As an example, a glut of milk developed despite falling production because the young families who normally purchased milk could no longer afford it. On the other hand, there was a tremendous boom in the manufacture of machines and the building of factories.

There was a vast increase in unproductive labour due to the complex calculations required in every trade, the continual conversions into foreign exchange, the application of complicated taxes, the computation of pay supplements, and the numerous economic controls. An actual shortage of bookkeepers developed. The ratio of office employees to production workers rose by 42% in nine years. Associated with this was a decline in the productivity of labour because of the diminution of real wages associated with a decline in the will to work. Many workmen found themselves just as well off not working. (This has once again been the case in Canada in the seventies). Productivity fell by close to 50%.

At first stock prices kept up with inflation, but after four years, they fell far behind. By 1922, stock prices had increased 89 times in price, while gold had gone up 1,525 times, and the consumer price index increased 945 times. This catastrophic drop in share prices produced strange situations. For example all the share capital of the Daimler car company was priced at the value of only 327 Daimler cars. Corporations reacted to this turn of events by creating special voting shares so as to protect control of their company. The reason stocks failed to keep up was that on December 1, 1921, the public was badly hit by a selling spree on the stock exchange and from that point, people became convinced that the only sure way to protect their savings was with gold or foreign exchange.

As Bresciani-Turroni put it:

> Expressed in paper marks the prices of shares seemed high. This exercised a psychological influence on the great mass of shareholders. Deluded by the apparently high prices, even the most cautious shareholders were induced to sell their securities; and only much later when the veil of inflation had been torn aside, did they realize that they had made a very bad bargain.

In the final phases of the inflation, stock prices again surged upwards because of the difficulty in obtaining gold and some shares actually became overvalued.

Another characteristic phenomenon of the inflation was the lessening of the differences between wages of different groups, skilled and unskilled, young and old, men and women. This was because as unskilled workers wages reached only subsistence levels, they were perforce increased, while the real wages of skilled workers were allowed to fall.

Stock holders who held their shares throughout the inflation lost 75% of their original investments. Mortgage and bond holders lost everything. In 1925, the German Government passed a law revaluing mortgages and debentures to 25% of their original gold value, but it proved almost totally impossible to enforce. Home owners who lived in their homes saved the investment in their homes and did not have to pay off the mortgage, but tenants fared even better, living for several years almost rent-free.

The group most seriously hurt by inflation were the professionals, especially doctors whose true incomes fell by 75%. In comparison government employees lost 50%. Consumption of better quality meats fell, while that of horses and dogs soared. Open prostitution increased as did the number of pawn shops.

It all ended in 1923 when the mark became worthless and the Government was forced back to gold to guarantee their new currency. In the aftermath came a credit crunch, 10% unemployment, and a severe depression followed by Adolph Hitler, but that is outside of the province of this book. What we must decide is how much of this scenario applies to us today.

Can Inflation Be Stopped?

Canada in 1980 is not like Germany of 1919. Canada is rich where Germany was poor. It has considerable reserves and borrowing power and has many more options open to it. Often I hear the comment "I'm not worried. The government will solve our problems if they get bad enough. They have the tools to do it."

Obviously all the advice in this book is worthless if some genius comes along and stops inflation and the slide of the dollar. Is this possible? The answer is an unequivocal *no, it is not possible.*

It is not individual or corporate spending that has driven us into inflation. It is governments who year after year have spent billions more than they have received and who in order to reverse this process must grossly cut their expenditures. But how do they do this? It is generally agreed that any massive cut in welfare will result in politically unacceptable violence in many cities.

Just as important, it is probably equally impossible for governments to encourage productivity when for two generations they have encouraged profligacy. People in government power talk about increasing productivity but they don't mean themselves or their own employees. The crazy thing is that while we have encouraged industry to produce more, for example it is great if a way can be found to increase one worker's output in a refrigeration factory from 31 refrigerators per week to 32, no one even dares suggest increasing the number òf students in each teacher's class from 31 to 32.

The gradual loss of productivity in government is well illustrated in my home of Ontario. The present "Conservative" Government came to power in 1943 when there were 2,300 civil servants in the province. Today, we are governed, not particularly better, by 80,000 civil servants. Periodically, the Government itself becomes alarmed at the increase in the number of its employees and puts a halt to hiring. But somehow the number of employees continues to grow as departments hire those people they think they need "by contract", instead of making them actual civil servants.

In 1978 the number of students enrolling in our schools fell drastically. As a result, there was a surplus of teachers. Rather than fire the extra teachers, the teachers' union and a group of popularity-seeking school trustees urged that instead we take this "great opportunity to raise standards" by decreasing the size of classes!

Although governments cannot, for political reasons, cut government spending and/or raise taxes to balance the budget and so stop inflation, they must *appear* to be doing something. In the U.S. and Canada this past year the "something" has been to raise interest rates. In the U.S. a new head was appointed to the Federal Reserve Board and this man raised U.S. interest rates by a whopping 50% over the past year, saying that something must be done to stop inflation.

Yet interest rates are just one more cost of doing business, like labour rates or the cost of raw materials, and the Federal Reserve Board statement that higher interest rates will stop inflation makes about as much sense as a union leader saying that increasing labour's wages will stop inflation! On November 28, 1979 the U.S. congress set American budget for the coming year to include a 30 billion dollar deficit. Any first-year economic student can tell that that means even more inflation and that higher interest rates will not affect the result one iota. What higher interest rates *do* produce is unemployment, because companies find it too expensive to borrow money which would finance expansion. In Canada we have been sheltered from the worst of the inflation by low fuel costs, but in 1980 the new Liberal government will definitely begin the process of removing that shelter. Once we pay the world price, or close to it, for oil, our inflation will move ahead rapidly and we can expect at least 15% by 1981.

The graph on page 38 foretells our financial doom. No politician is able to stop this inflation. No one in the United States or Canada is going to save the nation's financial health. All people can do is to protect their own finances so as to preserve the standard of living of their families.

What is the U.S. Government doing about the fall of the dollar?

For many years, the American Government just ignored the exchange rate of the U.S. dollar as it gradually sank. The Secretary of the Treasury in 1977 even expressed his

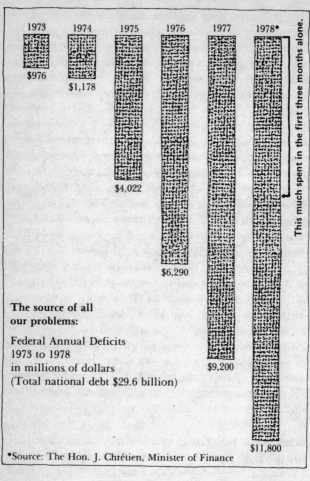

1973   1974   1975   1976   1977   1978*

$976

$1,178

$4,022

$6,290

$9,200

$11,800

This much spent in the first three months alone.

The source of all our problems:

Federal Annual Deficits
1973 to 1978
in millions of dollars
(Total national debt $29.6 billion)

*Source: The Hon. J. Chrétien, Minister of Finance

Canada's inflation is exactly the same as that in the United States, the only difference being that Canada is two years ahead in debasement of its dollar.

pleasure at this trend because it made American goods more competitive and reduced unemployment. Finally in October 1978, President Carter proclaimed that he intended to strengthen the U.S. dollar. He would auction off the U.S. gold reserve at the rate of 1,500,000 ounces per month. *The Wall Street Journal* called it the last throw of the dice.

By November 1979 it became obvious that the auction sales would not work and so the U.S. Treasury tried a new gimmick. They announced that in order to keep the gold buyers "off balance" they would give only three days notice of each auction and would not declare how much gold was to be sold until *after* the bidding was over!. Within a month of that announcement gold moved to over $500 an ounce.

I'd love to know who advised that crazy course of action. If the dollar is weak now with the gold in Fort Knox, *how* can it possibly be strengthened by selling off all of the only acceptable international currency belonging to the United States? It's exactly the same as a man going broke by overspending, who announces that he intends to continue his expenditures but will solve his problem by selling his house. When the money from the house is gone what does he do?

After Carter has sold the gold, he can try the various steps that Germany tried during its inflation. An obvious move would be to impose foreign exchange controls, forbidding U.S. citizens from owning gold or foreign currencies and restricting the amount of money carried by tourists. This would not solve the basic problem of government overspending, but it certainly would put off the day of final reckoning as the drain of private citizens selling dollars is curtailed.

In peacetime, however, such controls have never worked because enforcement is too difficult. Indeed such controls might have just the opposite results. They could initiate a wave of smuggling of currency out of the country for deposit in Switzerland, Germany, or Japan. Just a rumour of such controls in Canada in 1978 started a rush to export funds. Hundreds of millions of dollars from Canada were invested in the U.S. and overseas as a result.

Certainly an army of civil servants would be needed to enforce these new regulations. Everyone crossing the border would have to be searched and every letter going overseas would have to be opened. If the Mexican border can't be sealed to illegal immigrants, how can the entire U.S. be sealed to currency? I don't think the U.S. administration is stupid enough to try it. But if they do, it won't work.

Another route would be to follow the Canadian example and borrow vast amounts of foreign currency with which to purchase U.S. funds. This would temporarily sustain the trading price of the U.S. dollar. One hopes this would be done more intelligently than in Canada, where seven billion U.S. dollars, borrowed at an average of 8%, were used to prop up the Canadian dollar. Simultaneously, the Canadian Government loaned several billion dollars interest-free to third world countries as Canada's contribution to world development.

Such a policy won't work even in the short term, because the borrowed money is soon gone (it went at the rate of 300 million dollars a month in Canada) and the borrowing country is left owing the foreign currency which must be repaid someday and this in its turn forces the dollar lower. When the Canadian Government began borrowing to sustain the dollar, it stood at 89¢ U.S. Seven months and two billion dollars later, it had fallen below 85¢. The United States might try such a strategy, but it won't help.

A third option would be to impose strict import controls and drastically reduce the importation of foreign goods. This would rupture the U.S. foreign trade treaties and almost certainly produce a world-wide depression which could not be kept out of the United States. No, there is not much chance that this mistake will take place either.

There was one step that President Carter took that helped matters, at least temporarily. At the end of 1978 he ordered a *massive* raising of interest rates. With interest rates lower than the inflation rate, as they were throughout 1978, it made economic sense for speculators to borrow money to buy assets. This sped up the inflation and the Government realized that if it were to make money very expensive by raising the prime rate by several percentage points, it would become more difficult for borrowers and there would be some inflow of foreign currency to take advantage of the high interest. The effect can only be temporary, but both the U.S. and Canadian governments tried this strategy because they had so few other options. Higher interest rates, however, inevitably result in recession and high unemployment. Thus both governments will be forced to once again lower interest rates in 1980 and this will result in a sudden reacceleration of inflation followed by yet another raising of the interest rates. In the long term, interest rates *must* be higher than the inflation rate or gradually the private lenders stop making loans and buy assets instead. This vicious circle will result in even higher inflation and therefore even higher interest rates. I expect both to reach 25% per year by 1985.

A new factor came into the attack on the American dollar after the U.S. government froze all Iranian assets held in American banks. As *Barron's* put it on November 19, 1979:

The freeze of Iranian assets strikes us as a disaster the ugly implications of which have barely begun to sink in....Despite disclaimers to the contrary, confidence in the dollar among foreign holders has suffered a jolt. The freeze on Iranian assets, so one Arab diplomat was quoted as saying, sets a "worrisome" precedent. "It creates a nagging doubt. It's the same thing as choosing a bank for the degree of security it offers." Major creditors like the Saudis aren't apt to start a run on that bank — withdrawals, if they occur will doubtless be discreet and slow.

The problem is that every foreign government in the world is now aware that their deposits in the U.S. are at risk in case of a quarrel with that nation. Inevitably countries like Abu Dabai and Saudi Arabia will diversify their holdings elsewhere and that foretells new runs on the U.S. dollar, higher prices for gold and worse inflation.

How and when will inflation end? Every nation that has undergone prolonged serious inflation has seen it end in the same way, with an economic and political collapse. But that is many years away for Canadians and Americans, and it is not my purpose to speculate in this book where we will be in 1990. Instead I hope to enlighten the ordinary investor as to how to stay afloat during the next few years of inevitable, growing inflation.

Two Secrets to Profit During Inflation

There are two secrets to financial success in inflationary periods. They are:

(1) Buy equity — things that will go up in value as the dollar loses its buying power.
(2) Use borrowed money.

Secret #1: Buy Equity

During inflation, we have seen that paper investments, such as bonds, mortgages, and insurance, lose their value because they don't go up in pace with inflation. We must therefore buy real objects — equity — which will rise in value. Where is the most *profit* to be made?

It is true that all real objects go up in price as the dollar goes down in value, but for investment purposes it is easy to eliminate most things. For example, it doesn't matter if butter is going to double in price over the next year. Obviously we are not going to fill our homes with butter because of storage and resale problems. The butter will all have gone bad long before any profit is possible. Similarly, we should not invest in anything which has a large discrepancy between the bidding and asking price. The buyer should be able to immediately resell his purchase at almost the same price. That is why it would be foolish to go to a jewellery store and buy expensive rings as a hedge against inflation. It may be true that those rings will move up 25% in price this next year because of inflation, but the purchaser has probably paid a 60% mark-up to the retailer.

The two problems of storage and net value eliminate most objects as protection from inflation. (It is a difficult concept for many people to accept — my wife still thinks she's protecting our assets from inflation every time she visits Saks 5th Avenue.) What is left?

real estate
commodities
gold and other precious metals
some stocks
art and antiques
wine
old stamps, coins, books and rugs
memorabilia

The problem with all of these is that in themselves they cannot protect us from the ravages of inflation. The reason is simply this. Suppose you are forty years old with a family and a good job bringing in $35,000 per year. Your life savings are $50,000. You invest your $50,000 in one of the above inflation-proof categories, for example gold, and over the next five years, there is a 100% inflation and the gold goes up 100% in value to $100,000. Your standard of living, however, still falls. Although the gold has gone up enough to preserve the true value of your savings, this has done nothing about the falling value of your salary which is not inflation proof and which is most unlikely to go up as fast as the inflation. We must now understand the second secret.

Secret #2: Borrowed Money

Buying equity helps *keep up* with inflation, but the only way to *get ahead* of inflation is through the use of borrowed money. Let us take the same example. With the same assets and the same income, you now borrow an extra $50,000 using your own $50,000 as security and buy $100,000 worth of gold. At the end of five years your $100,000 worth of gold is worth $200,000. After you have paid back the $50,000 you borrowed plus the interest, you have $125,000 left. You have crept ahead of inflation!

It only makes sense to borrow money if that money can be borrowed at less than the inflation rate, so obviously one should not go to a loan shark or even a finance company. In fact, in only two fields of investment is it simple and cheap for the ordinary person to borrow long term money: real estate and commodities. These are the two areas where huge profits will be made during inflation.

Is Equity Always the Thing to Buy?

There is one important point to remember about equity. Keep away from buying items retail which have a large spread between retail and wholesale prices. There is no profit to be made in buying a print at $100 retail, seeing it appreciate over five years to $200 retail, and then going back to the gallery where you bought it and being offered only its $100 wholesale value. I think that everyone understands that an object sold in any store is marked up anywhere from 50 to 100% and that only a fool would buy retail as an investment. Even though this appears obvious, it's surprising how many people forget this truism if the salesman is clever and the object is dressed up.

A perfect example is the sale of diamonds. Millions of dollars worth of diamonds have been sold at inflated prices over the past five years to people who should know better. It seems obvious enough that when De Beers marks raw diamonds up 20% to their wholesaler, and the wholesaler in turn marks them up another 30% to the distributor, and the distributor adds about $1/_3$ on his sale to the jeweller and the jeweller adds 60 to 75% before the customer sees them, that it is going to take a pretty big move in diamond prices before the last man in the chain can sell at a profit. And yet very profitable high pressure advertising and phone campaigns have succeeded in loading up thousands of simple people with quantities of diamonds as a spurious inflation hedge.

The pitch is remarkably simple. One firm reprinted this table showing price increases received by the De Beers diamond trust since 1966.

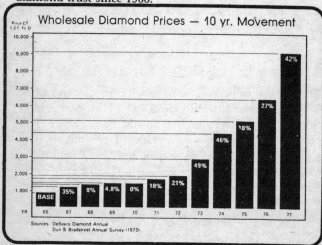

They then went on to tell potential customers:

In this age of financial uncertainty, it's comforting to know that one investment medium has continued to rise calmly through good times and bad. Since the 1930's, the price of diamonds at the producer level has risen steadily with no declines on any year-to-year basis. . . .Reasons we believe diamond prices will continue to rise,

(1) Supplies are dwindling while demand is growing.
(2) Diamond prices automatically adjust for inflation.
(3) Mining costs continue to rise.
(4) Political difficulties in Southern Africa.

Jewelry demand for diamonds is currently consuming most everything that's being produced. Added to this, burgeoning investment demand provides additional upward impetus.

Well, maybe — but there is no question that an awful lot of promoters are making a pretty good living selling diamonds in just this way!

Don't buy diamonds. There is little chance of profit even if the price goes up. Twenty-five years ago my wife purchased a diamond bracelet for $1,500 and, as it is now out of fashion and diamond prices are supposed to have gone up tenfold last year, she decided to sell. She discovered to her dismay that in the last ten years diamonds are cut in a different way and as her diamonds are "old cut" they are now worth $1,500! This is hardly the best inflation hedge.

Equity is useless as an inflation hedge unless you are buying at the *real* (wholesale) value. So forget about diamonds, old cars, prints or anything else if you are buying retail. But it is neither necessary to be in the business nor to be an expert to buy equity wholesale. More about that later.

Real Estate

Houses

Unquestionably, the first investment anyone should make in times of inflation is a house. It should be the most expensive home you can afford with the biggest mortgage on which you can meet the payments.

There are many reasons to begin with a home:

(1) A house is easily bought with someone else's money using a mortgage.
(2) Governments tend to avoid taxing profits on homes because there are so many voting homeowners.
(3) In some jurisdictions, mortgage interest is deductible from your income tax.
(4) You completely control the course of the investment, unlike a stock in which you are at the mercy of management.
(5) Housing prices tend to rise faster than the general inflation rate. As inflation progresses and rent control spreads, a shortage of rental accommodations will develop, producing upward pressure on housing prices.

My secretary carried the manoeuvre out perfectly. Ann is 44, married with two children. She and her husband Russ have worked all their lives and in 1966, they took their life savings of $8,000 and bought a beautiful home for $46,500, paying for it with a government-guaranteed twenty-year 6¾% mortgage. Twelve years later, they still owed $30,000 on the mortgage, but because of inflation that $46,500 house was now worth about $250,000. Their equity was about $220,000. Note that it is not $46,500 that has grown to $220,000. All Ann and Russ put in was $8,000, and that $8,000 has grown to $220,000 *with no taxes* on the profits. In no other way could any profit be made without taxation. And in no other way could an ordinary individual turn an $8,000 investment into $220,000 in twelve years.

This is just the beginning. As inflation speeds up, that $250,000 house could easily sell for a million dollars in six or seven years from now. This is a perfect example of how to profit from inflation.

When buying a house, don't worry about the interest rate on the mortgage so long as you can meet the payments. Interest rates always lag behind the inflation rate. More important, the mortgage rate remains constant throughout the life of the mortgage even though the inflation rate will continue to climb. Anyone today can repeat what Ann did twelve years ago. The only difference is that the numbers are higher. Today, first mortgages are available at 12 to 14% and if you buy a house with such a mortgage you are really not paying any true interest at all. The reason is that the buying power of the dollar is shrinking at the same rate, so that in effect the mortgage holder is loaning you his money interest free.

Furthermore if one looks down the road five or ten years, the $50,000 or $100,000 mortgage you place now with today's dollars will be paid off when it comes due with vastly depreciated money. $50,000 today will buy an airplane. In ten years, I doubt it will buy a Cadillac. The result will be that the mortgage holder will have given a present of the house to you, the buyer.

I cannot stress it strongly enough. If you do not already own your own home, *buy it now!*

Rental Properties

Other types of real estate are a different matter. Probably the worst investment anyone could make today would be to buy an apartment house, or duplex or any type of rental property. The reason is that governments come under intense pressure during inflation to "do something" and one very popular thing to do is to freeze rents. There are a hundred tenants for every landlord in the electorate and it becomes irresistable for a politician to take this foolish but expedient move. I suspect that most politicians know that this is a mistake which inevitably results in a deterioration and shortage of housing. But try to explain that to an angry electorate squeezed by rising prices and falling true income. It is easier for the politician just to give in and let his successor worry about the problems which inevitably follow.

Much of Canada and the United States already has rent control and many areas are blighted as a result but there is no doubt that as inflation gets worse rent control will spread further. Those immediately hurt are the investors.

Barely a hundred miles from my home, on the east side of Buffalo is a perfect example of the end results of rent control. As costs rose but rents remained frozen, housing maintenance gradually stopped and neighbourhoods deteriorated. Finally, it no longer made financial sense to pay the taxes and one owner after another simply walked away from their investments. Today, a lot can be purchased in that part of Buffalo for $100. For $200, one can buy a lot with a house.

Don't buy rental income. It's a trap!

Farmland

Farms come in a special category of their own and represent an excellent investment today, second only to a family home. The farm represents a good investment for four reasons:

(1) Farmland goes up in price like everything else in inflationary times.
(2) Farms can be bought with someone else's money, using a mortgage.
(3) As cities grow, farmland gradually disappears and the remaining land becomes more valuable.
(4) Farms grow food and while consumption of everything else will fall as inflation speeds up because of the general population's falling income, farmland has an extra value because everyone must eat.

If you buy a farm, do so with the largest, longest running mortgage you can arrange and afford. In 1974, I purchased a 67 acre farm twenty miles outside of Toronto, paying $225,000 with $75,000 down and a $150,000 mortgage. In the five years that mortgage has already run, the dollar has lost 40% of its buying power. The $150,000 now represents only $100,000 in terms of buying power.

There are land taxes to pay on farmland. Though the taxes tend to be low, it is advisable, wherever possible, to rent your land to a farmer. This will bring in enough income to at least cover the taxes.

Three warnings:

(1) There is always the danger of governments initiating special taxes on profits made on land held for speculation. Ontario did this in 1974, effectively cracking the land market. Don't buy land anywhere if a future change towards this type of taxation is a possibility.

(2) Never buy any type of land that is far away from your home. There are innumerable sharpees selling inaccessible scrub in northern Ontario, described as lush vacation property to foolish Americans, while Canadians are plagued by sellers of ocean front Florida properties accessible only at low tide. If you are going to buy land, buy it within easy driving distance of your home.

(3) Real estate has the disadvantage of lack of liquidity. You can't get out in a hurry. A family home is an excellent inflation investment, but after that investment is made you will probably do better looking elsewhere for your second venture.

Commodities

Commodities are anything grown from or found in the ground, including cocoa, coffee, orange juice, cattle, copper, gold, sugar, cotton, hogs, platinum, and silver.

Dealing in commodities is gambling, and commodity trading cannot be indulged in unless you have money you can afford to lose. But commodities are one of the few places left where you have a chance of making a fortune from a few thousand dollars. The reason is the huge leverage. A trader puts down only 5 or 10% of the purchase price and thus a 5 or 10% move either doubles his stake or wipes it out entirely.

Commodities respond to innumerable pressures varying from the weather in Ghana to the supply of anchovies in Peru, from the state of health of Anwar Sadat to the success of rebels in Zaire. All the factors resulting in the price of any one commodity can never be known to any individual. This produces the excitement in commodity trading. No one knows for sure what will happen next and the intelligent amateur has as much chance as the huge multi-national traders.

The two requirements for a commodity to be traded must be:

(1) a fluctuating price;
(2) storability.

Commodity trading originally began as a way for farmers to sell their crop at a guaranteed price long before harvest time, and thereby guarantee themselves a profit. Also, it was a route whereby manufacturers could contract to buy their raw material in advance so as to be protected against future jumps in price. Over the years, speculators came in to the market to fill the gap when there was no buyer or seller, guaranteeing both farmer and manufacturer a profit and attempting in the process to make money for themselves. Only 20% succeed in making money, but it is fairly easy to be in that 20%.

Commodities trade on an exchange just as do stocks, but there are important differences between commodities and stocks:

(1) Commodities have very low margins.
(2) Commodities have low commissions; about 1/10 of that on an equivalent amount of stock.
(3) Commodities must be paid for with cash in advance. If you buy a stock you have five days to pay.
(4) When buying stock, you say, "Buy me 100 shares of AT & T". Commodities however, trade in units and each unit varies with the commodity. Gold is 100 ounces, sugar is 112,000 pounds, cattle is 40,000 pounds. If you say, "Buy me three cattle," you are ordering the purchase of 120,000 pounds of cattle.
(5) Unlike stocks, each commodity has a daily "limit" to its price changes. Whereas a stock may plunge or soar on bad or good news, commodities are only

allowed to move a certain amount each day. Cattle may not move up or down more than 1½¢ from the previous day's close (but remember that 1½¢ represents $600 per contract). These limit moves are great if the commodity is moving in the direction you have invested but if it is going the other way it can be very painful not to be able to sell out and take your loss.

Can the ordinary investor make money from commodities and if so how? There is a well written and amusing book on investments terribly mistitled *The Only Investment Guide You'll Ever Need** which starts out by saying keep away from the commodity market because 80% of the players lose. The author finally works himself up to quote a study of 1000 commodity traders in which not one made money. If all these suckers are losing, who is making that money? It's people like me.

In 1975, I made $4,400 net in the commodity market. In 1976, I made $48,200 and in 1977, $56,000. In 1978, I made $60,500 and in 1979 I made $195,500. If anyone thinks I'm not telling the truth, you are welcome to inspect my trading account at the firm where I do my commodity trading: Friedberg & Co., 347 Bay Street, Toronto. I have achieved this by spending no more than 15 minutes per day at commodities.

Nor am I some unique genius. In fact, my winnings are small potatoes compared to what some people have taken out of the commodity market since inflation sped up three years ago. The reason my earnings are comparatively small is that I don't like to gamble. I limit my holdings to a maximum of twenty diversified contracts at any one time.

*Andrew Tobias. Harcourt, Brace, Jovanovich, 1978.

Well what are the secrets?

First of all let's go back to the inflation. What goes up in an inflation? Everything! And commodities represent everything. Whether you look at silver or cocoa, cattle or orange juice, almost all commodities are selling at higher prices than they were five years ago. It's true that they don't all go up at the same time or the same pace and some are going down while others are going up. But the overall trend is up. The following rules are important for commodity trading:

(1) *Go with the trend. Buy commodities.* Don't trade on the short side. Leave that to the professionals.

(2) *Be prepared to take many small losses, but maximize your profits.* As soon as you are down 25% of your deposit, accept your loss and sell out. Let profits ride for the maximum time allowed in the contract. In 1973, I added up all my trades for the year and found that I had lost in 92 transactions and profited in only 12. However, I still showed a net profit of $14,000 for the year.

(3) *Don't buy into commodities that have had huge upward price surges.* The inevitable correction may wipe you out before you get started. If you really feel like gambling this is one time where selling something short can prove very profitable. My activity sheet for June 1977, which appears at the top of page 59, illustrates these points.

In May 1977, coffee had a huge price surge going all the way from 50¢ to $3 following a freeze in Brazil. This $3 wholesale price translated into $6 coffee in the supermarkets and there was a lot of press and threats of consumer boycott. It was fairly obvious coffee prices were going to come back down. On May 20, I sold a coffee contract at $2.89. I was able to buy the coffee back on June 3 at $2.44 giving me a profit of $16,875. On the other hand, in the

DATE	BOUGHT	SOLD	COMMODITY	PRICE		
**** CONFIRMATIONS FOLLOW *******						
			BEGINNING LEDGER BAL.	4,728.14		
77-06-03	1		77JUL COFFEE NY.	258.50		
77-06-03	1		78MAR COFFEE NY.	244.00		
77-06-03	1		77OCT PLATINUM	156.00		
77-06-03	1		77AUG GOLD-COMEX	142.20		
**** PURCHASES AND SALES FOLLOW ******						
77-06-02	1		77JUL COFFEE NY.	263.50		
77-06-03		1*	77JUL COFFEE NY.	258.50 P&S	1,875.00	
77-06-03	1		78MAR COFFEE NY.	289.00		
77-06-03		1*	78MAR COFFEE NY.	244.00 P&S		16,875.00
77-05-20		1*	77OCT PLATINUM	163.10		
77-06-03	1		77OCT PLATINUM	156.00 P&S	355.00	
77-05-26		1*	77AUG GOLD-COMEX	144.20		
77-06-03	1		77AUG GOLD-COMEX	142.20 P&S	200.00	
			TOTAL TOTAL GROSS P OR L			
			TOTAL FEES & COMMISSIONS		302.00	
			NET P OR L *			
			TOTAL ADJ			
			TOTAL NET CHANGE **			14,445.00
			NEW LEDGER BALANCE **			14,143.00
						14,143.00
						9,414.86

other three trades shown, one in coffee, one in platinum and one in gold, as soon as things began to go against me, I took my loss. I ended up losing in three out of four transactions, but still ended up with a net profit of $14,143 for the period.

(4) *Choose a reliable broker.* It is amazing how many villains and dolts are in this field. Ask your would-be broker two questions: (1) Do you also personally handle stock trading? (2) Is your firm a member of the Chicago Mercantile Exchange or the Board of Trade? If he answers yes to the first or no to the second, try somewhere else. To do well, you need someone who specializes in this very tough field and you must take care not to link up with some fly-by-night firm that won't be there when pay-out time comes.

(5) *Pyramiding is the way to make big profits from small investments.* This is the means by which one uses one's profits to buy more of the same commodity as it moves, without putting in any more money. Opposite is an example of pyramiding.

Note that on November 15, I sold four Canadian dollar contracts at prices between $85.07 and $85.25. By December 11, the dollar was down to $84.94 and I sold two more contracts, and continued to build my pyramid right through to January 31, when the dollar closed at $83.36. By this time I had a paper profit of $13,160 and was short twelve Canadian dollar contracts representing $1,200,000. This is the smart way to trade commodities, building a pyramid and expanding your position if it goes in the right direction.

(6) *It is essential to be well informed in this or any other investment.* The basics are published daily in *The Wall Street Journal,* Toronto's *Globe and Mail,* and many other financially oriented newspapers. A subscription to at least one of these is essential.

In addition all commodity brokers distribute to their clients a market letter. The big firms, such as Merrill Lynch, sometimes send out a daily letter on *each* active

DATE	BOUGHT	SOLD	COMMODITY	TRADE PRICE	SETTLEMENT PRICE	DEBIT	CREDIT
			BEGINNING LEDGER BALANCE			4,616.61	
79/01/03	1	1	79JUN GINNIE MAE				1,112.50
79/01/08		1	79JUN GINNIE MAE				456.25
79/01/08	2	2	79MAR OR.JUICE				1,145.00
79/01/10	3	3	79MAR JAP.YEN				
79/01/26	CASH DISB					4,005.00	
79/01/26	2	2	79MAR CAN.DLRS.			3,000.00	
**** OPEN TRADES FOLLOW ****							4,180.00
78/11/15	1		79MAR CAN.DLRS.	85.07	83.36		1,710.00
78/11/15	1		79MAR CAN.DLRS.	85.15	83.36		1,790.00
78/11/15	1		79MAR CAN.DLRS.	85.23	83.36		1,870.00
78/11/15	1		79MAR CAN.DLRS.	85.25	83.36		1,890.00
78/12/08	1		79MAR CAN.DLRS.	85.13	83.36		1,770.00
78/12/08	1		79MAR CAN.DLRS.	84.94	83.36		1,580.00
78/12/19	1		79MAR CAN.DLRS.	84.52	83.36		960.00
79/01/02	1		79MAR CAN.DLRS.	84.10	83.36		740.00
79/01/17	1		79MAR CAN.DLRS.	84.02	83.36		660.00
79/01/17	1		79MAR CAN.DLRS.	83.75	83.36	160.00	390.00
79/01/31	1		79MAR CAN.DLRS.	83.20	83.36	40.00	
79/01/31	1		79MAR CAN.DLRS.	83.52	83.36		
		12					
78/12/26	1		79MAR GOLD-IMM	218.80	234.50		13,160.00
78/12/28	1		79MAR GOLD-IMM	228.30	234.50		1,570.00
79/01/02	1		79MAR GOLD-IMM	227.90	234.50		620.00
79/01/17	1		79MAR GOLD-IMM	236.50	234.50	210.00	400.00
79/01/25	1		79MAR GOLD-IMM	236.00	234.50		
	5						
				OPEN TRADE EQUITY			3,040.00
				LEDGER BALANCE			16,200.00
				TOTAL EQUITY **		4,727.86	11,472.14

	MARGIN--MTD		
	INIT	MAINT	
	36500	28000	

commodity but that is a little more information than the dabbler (like myself) really wants. One of the very best market letters that consistently has given good advice is that sent out gratis to his customers by my broker, Friedberg & Co. Friedberg is a small firm that accepts no new small clients, but it is possible to subscribe to the newsletter.

If you really want to be on top of things you can rent a ticker tape from Translux Corporation for $125 per month (plus another $60 to the Chicago Mercantile Exchange or Currency Exchange), which will show you every trade simultaneously as it occurs. (Just for fun, I briefly put one in my office, but it was too diverting from my medical practice.)

(7) *Try to go against the popular view.* It is a good rule of thumb that once the price of a commodity reaches the front page of *The New York Times,* it's time to get out. When sugar hit 65¢, five years ago, the newspaper stories said that it was going to $1 per pound and the same happened with coffee in 1977. Remember that the public is always wrong.

(8) Buy commodities that in terms of real money have not gone up much in the past decade. If you bear in mind that the cost of living has more than doubled in the past twelve years and compare the prices of commodities then and now you will see that some things are selling at a lower price today compared to twelve years ago relative to all other prices. These commodities are orange juice, cotton, zinc, copper, broilers and hogs. Any speculator buying these commodities at current prices is running very little risk.

(9) Gold is a special situation that will be discussed in the next chapter.

Before leaving commodities, I should point out that they can move up or down in price very, very rapidly and this quick action produces an excitement that some people just can't handle. The sort of person who can't sleep because he goes over and over in his mind what he should have done should never enter the commodities field.

If you don't have the time to give to commodity trading (unlike stocks, commodities must be watched very closely), but still want to put some of your money into this field, then consideration should be given to a *commodity fund*. These funds allow speculators with as little as $1,000 to put money into several commodities at once. The way it works is that a brokerage house will set up a million-dollar cash fund by selling 1,000 units at $1,000 each. This money is then invested in a broad cross-section of commodities, so that each investor's $1,000 is divided up proportionally to the funds total assets.

Some of these funds have done remarkably well. A recent analysis by *The Wall Street Journal* showed that one such fund grew from $30,000 in 1972 to over $700,000 in 1978. They don't all do well, however, and *The Journal* found one commodity fund that dropped by 50% in just two years. *The Wall Street Journal* summed it up this way:

The trading managers' past performance suggests that the systems will, at worst, lose investors' money a good deal slower than amateur speculators can lose it on their own, and at best, earn such speculators a great deal more money than they could earn themselves. That is a major reason why professional commodities management has become attractive to risk-tolerant investors in the past few years.

Thomson McKinnon and Shearson Hayden Stone are two New York firms offering such a service.

What bothers me most about such funds is that all of their investment decisions are made by a computer which attempts from past prices and trading to analyze what is going to happen. Such a method ignores all basic changes in supply and demand, current economic developments or even a sudden war which might drastically affect a commodity. I am very uneasy about computer trading. On the other hand, it is the only way to get into the commodity market with only $1,000 to start. (I should mention that the broker will ask his customer to sign a statement that he or she has a net worth of $50,000 or a yearly income over $20,000.)

Some of the smaller commodity firms have set up mutual funds in which they charge $2,500 per share and many of these have been spectacularly successful. Here is the record as of the end of 1978 of the nine funds set up by one Toronto commodity broker from March 1976 to March 1978:

Name of Limited Partnership	Date Begun	Initial Capital	Date Ended	Capital at end of Sept. 78	% Change
Commtor I	Mar. 76	C$59,000	Mar. 77	C$173,374.45	+193.9
Commtor 1977	Mar. 77	159,000	Mar. 78	407,422.00	+156.2
Dealcom	Apr. 77	83,000	Apr. 78	96,198.35	+ 15.9
Zeifcom	May 77	75,000		140,080.96	+ 86.8
Olive	Oct. 77	160,000		233,312.39	+ 45.8
Marten	Oct. 77	127,000		175,866.83	+ 38.5
Nosegay	Dec. 77	78,000		212,499.85	+172.4
Commtor 1978	Feb. 78	350,000		502,111.91	+ 43.5
Stoat	Mar. 78	99,500		119,563.98	+ 20.2

(The particular company running the funds does not solicit new clients for its funds and has asked me not to use their name).

I really think the clever speculator is better off on his own. But if someone is nervous about starting, this is a relatively painless way to do it, although it is definitely a second choice. In my opinion, using a computer to pick an investment is just a modern version of charting.

The Mindless Guide to Investment

There is a belief widely held that if one carefully studies the past price movements of a commodity (or stock or currency), one will be able to predict its future price changes. Believers in this method carefully make charts of the daily (and sometimes hourly) prices and volumes at which their stock trades and by studying the chart or picture this produces they think that they can tell what is about to happen. The theory on which charting is based is this: No one can possibly know all the factors affecting the price changes of any security, but the market knows because all the individual buy and sell forces are exposed in the trading of that security. Furthermore the pull in both directions will be clearly reflected in the way stock prices move up or down. Invariably the same factors that produce a chart showing one picture will result in an upward price movement, while the factors that will end up in a downward price change shows quite a different chart.

This theory of chart investments is nonsensical. It has always amazed me how many followers charts have. *No chart can foretell what price changes will occur tomorrow.* How could a chart know that a freeze is going to hit Brazil causing coffee price to soar? I strongly urge my readers to ignore such a foolish nostrum.

And incidentally there are other people, including stock advisors, who make their investments on the basis of the stars, their horoscope, hunches, hot tips or even what they see in the funnies. To all of these hopefuls I can only say good luck, for rationality is lost upon them.

Follow these rules and you can take advantage of inflation instead of it taking advantage of you.

But remember this: the best trader following the most sensible rules will get clobbered occasionally in the commodity market. Don't enter this field unless you can afford to lose. For those seeking safety there are far better places to put your money—like gold.

Commodities

JANUARY 31, 1980

Symbols for the exchange on which each commodity is traded appear in brackets after the commodity, followed by the minimum contract size and the monetary units used in the table. Open interest is the number of contracts outstanding each month and not liquidated by delivery of the commodity or by an offsetting contract.

Exchanges: CBT—Chicago Board of Trade, KCBT—Kansas City Board of Trade, CME—Chicago Mercantile Exchange, NYCSE—New York Coffee and Sugar Exchange, NYC-TN—New York Cotton Exchange, NYM—New York Mercantile Exchange, NYCX—Commodity Exchange in New York, NYCO—New York Cocoa Exchange, IMM—International Monetary Market of the Chicago Mercantile Exchange.

METALS

—Season— High	Low		High	Low	Close	Chg.	Open Int.
PLATINUM (NYM)—50 troy oz.; $ per troy oz.							
905.00	905.00	Feb	811.00	810.00	811.00	+ 3.00	32
960.00	790.00	Mar	815.00	815.00	815.00		0
974.40	278.80	Apr	837.00	807.00	832.00	+ 4.00	3825
977.30	315.40	Jul	850.00	820.00	846.00	+ 11.50	2252
983.80	378.00	Oct	870.00	835.00	862.00	+ 16.00	1307
987.20	388.00	Jan	878.00	863.00	872.00	+ 18.50	808
Est. sales 1,554; sales Wed. 1,648.							
Total open interest Wed. 8,224 off 125 from Tues.							
SILVER (CBT)—5,000 troy oz.; ¢ per troy oz.							
4145.0	541.00	Feb	3600 0 3460.0		3550.0	- 57.00	3509
4177.0	2855.0	Mar			3595.0	- 43.00	1
4212.0	573.50	Apr	3660 0	3590.0	3610.0	- 60.00	4167
4259.0	588.00	Jun	3725.0	3652.0	3670.0	- 62.00	3886
3795.0	600.00	Aug	3765.0	3694.0	3740.0	- 34.00	3122
4170.5	637.00	Oct	3807.0	3736.0	3762.0	- 54.00	3796
4235.0	656.00	Dec			3802.0	- 56.00	3168
4184.0	670.20	Feb			3842.0	- 58.00	5597
4240.0	698.00	Apr			3882.0	- 60.00	7885
4005.0	713.00	Jun			3922.0	- 62.00	5206
4450.0	737.00	Aug	4038.0	3954.0	3962.0	- 72.00	4911
4095.0	850.90	Oct			4002.0	- 74.00	1214
4140.0	894.00	Dec			4042.0	- 76.00	945
4190.0	927.50	Feb			4082.0	- 78.00	947
4265.0	1030.5	Apr			4122.0	- 80.00	1022
4278.0	1043.5	Jun			4164.0	- 80.00	1025
4320.0	1260.0	Aug	4206.0	4206.0	4206.0	- 80.00	413
Est. sales 1,466; sales Wed. 1,728.							
Total open interest Wed. 50,482, off 606 from Tues.							

—Season— High	Low		High	Low	Close	Chg.	Open Int.
COPPER (NYCX)—25,000 lb.; ¢ per lb.							
133.50	73.80	Feb	130.00	129.00	128.75	- 3.55	88
138.90	73.80	Mar	131.60	129.30	130.50	- 3.30	18263
140.80	75.55	May	132.70	130.50	131.60	- 3.20	18243
142.50	73.80	Jul	133.50	131.00	132.40	- 3.40	8770
143.50	73.80	Sep	133.90	131.60	132.80	- 3.50	1307
144.50	80.70	Dec	134.80	132.70	133.40	- 3.60	5965
145.00	81.20	Jan	134.10	134.00	133.70	- 3.60	284
145.90	81.00	Mar	135.40	133.30	134.20	- 3.60	3894
146.80	81.40	May	100.00	134.50	134.70	- 3.60	2857
147.70	89.10	Jul	136.70	136.00	135.20	- 3.60	947
148.60	96.60	Sep	137.00	136.30	135.70	- 3.60	696
138.50	137.00	Dec	137.50	137.00	136.40	- 3.60	1
Est. sales 9,800; sales Wed. 9,574.							
Total open interest Wed. 63,315 up 288 from Tues.							
GOLD (IMM)—100 troy oz.; $ per troy oz.							
705.00	667.00	Feb	690.00	639.00	685.00	+ 17.00	133
880.50	210.50	Mar	702.00	643.00	693.00	+ 19.00	8529
914.50	226.00	Jun	732.00	675.00	728.50	+ 21.00	13369
938.00	231.70	Sep	764.00	707.00	758.50	+ 18.50	8446
957.50	262.50	Dec	791.00	745.00	790.50	+ 19.00	1363
976.00	282.20	Mar	825.00	780.00	820.50	+ 18.50	1905
993.90	351.70	Jun	850.00	810.00	849.50	+ 18.00	1145
1011.20	455.90	Sep	878.50	845.00	878.50	+ 18.50	232
1031.90	794.40	Dec	907.00	870.00	907.00	+ 19.50	92
Est. sales 10,064; sales Wed. 9,396.							
Total open interest Wed. 41,014, off 1,085 from Tues.							

SILVER (NYCX)—5,000 troy oz.; ¢ per troy oz.

Season High	Season Low	Month	High	Low	Close	Chg.	Open Int.
3600.00	2295.00	Feb	3510.0	3420.0	3460.0	−125.0	4
4150.00	582.00	Mar	3625.0	3575.0	3575.0	− 75.0	13060
4150.00	582.00	Apr			3600.0	− 75.0	0
4100.00	610.50	May	3700.0	3625.0	3625.0	− 75.0	12680
4240.00	642.40	Jul	3665.0	3665.0	3665.0	− 75.0	11736
4280.00	666.00	Sep			3710.0	− 75.0	11736
4437.00	796.00	Dec	3765.0	3765.0	3764.5	− 75.0	10532
3688.00	843.50	Jan			3783.0	− 75.0	6743
4493.50	924.00	Mar			3821.0	− 75.0	7075
4530.50	1006.00	May			3859.0	− 75.0	3050
4267.50	1257.00	Jul			3897.0	− 75.0	1180
3904.50	1885.90	Sep			3935.0	− 75.0	353

Est. sales 300; sales Wed. 981.
Total open interest Wed. 78,393 off 213 from Tues.

GOLD (NYCX)—100 troy oz.; $ per troy oz.

Season High	Season Low	Month	High	Low	Close	Chg.	Open Int.
840.50	190.50	Feb	687.00	638.00	681.50	+23.50	4499
847.50	530.00	Mar	695.00	661.00	692.50	+23.00	65
854.80	212.00	Apr	708.00	658.00	704.00	+23.00	23887
869.00	225.00	Jun	730.00	679.00	726.00	+22.50	20392
882.70	229.50	Aug	755.00	703.50	748.00	+22.50	18054
896.30	236.50	Oct	778.00	725.00	769.00	+22.50	16999
909.90	270.30	Dec	805.08	745.00	789.50	+22.00	25644
873.70	276.50	Feb	812.00	765.00	809.00	+22.00	23661
886.50	322.50	Apr	836.50	786.00	828.50	+22.00	21293
899.50	324.00	Jun	850.00	804.00	848.00	+22.00	8425
900.00	442.00	Aug	844.00	844.00	867.50	+22.00	8669
1026.4	557.50	Oct	880.00	848.00	887.00	+22.00	1528

Est. sales 26,000; sales Wed. 30,114.
Total open interest Wed. 173,265 off 4,032 from Tues.

FOODS

COFFEE (NYCSE)—37,500 lb.; ¢ per lb.

Season High	Season Low	Month	High	Low	Close	Chg.	Open Int.
217.05	111.50	Mar	166.50	163.65	166.39	+ 1.39	3513
216.49	116.00	May	171.60	168.25	171.00	+ 1.00	4953
215.65	149.25	Jul	176.25	173.50	176.21	+ 1.21	1742
214.78	168.50	Sep	178.50	176.00	178.38	+ 0.88	1429
199.50	172.94	Dec	177.00	174.70	176.95	+ 0.87	673
199.00	168.25	May	175.50	173.50	175.30	+ 0.30	404
179.99	168.00	May	175.50	174.90	174.63	− 0.04	75

Est. sales 4,305; sales Wed. 4,919.
Total open interest Wed. 12,789 up 237 from Tues.
Parana spot 2.00n

EGGS, Shell (CME)—22,500 doz.; ¢ per doz.

Season High	Season Low	Month	High	Low	Close	Chg.	Open Int.
58.25	44.25	Feb	45.15	44.25	44.25	− 2.00	16
59.25	51.10	Mar	51.65	51.10	51.10	− .50	37
59.00	48.90	Apr	49.65	48.90	48.90	− .60	12
54.00	49.50	May		50.20	49.90	50.00	14

Est. sales 17; sales Wed. 19.
Total open interest Wed. 79, up 4 from Tues.

ORANGE JUICE (NYCTN)—15,000 lb.; ¢ per lb.

Season High	Season Low	Month	High	Low	Close	Chg.	Open Int.
118.50	85.90	Mar	89.70	88.50	88.85	+ 1.85	3681
113.75	87.00	May	90.00	89.00	89.65	+ 1.75	1581
111.50	88.50	Jul	91.20	90.00	90.80	+ 1.50	962
109.30	90.40	Sep	92.60	91.70	92.20	+ 1.80	701
99.00	92.50	Nov			92.80	+ 0.80	16
107.75	90.50	Jan	92.00	90.50	91.50	+ 0.70	307
96.00	91.10	Mar	92.40	91.10	92.40	+ 0.80	122
97.50	92.00	May	92.25	92.00	93.15	+ 0.55	17

Est. sales 1,400; sales Wed. 606.
Total open interest Wed. 7,506 off 90 from Tues.

SUGAR, World (NYCSE)—112,000 lb.; ¢ per lb.

Season High	Season Low	Month	High	Low	Close	Chg.	Open Int.
22.05	9.12	Mar	22.05	20.90	22.01	+ 0.95	18822
21.14	9.34	May	21.14	21.00	21.97	+ 1.00	32429
22.14	9.60	Jul	22.14	21.25	22.14	+ 1.00	27704
22.24	9.85	Sep	22.24	21.42	22.24	+ 1.00	6694
22.26	10.03	Oct	22.40	21.40	22.26	+ 1.00	11307
22.40	19.14	Jan	22.40	21.70	22.10	+ 0.70	31
22.42	13.73	Mar	22.42	21.65	22.38	+ 0.96	3655
22.40	15.61	May	22.40	21.70	22.28	+ 0.78	2841

Est. sales 28,750; sales Wed. 14,189.
Total open interest Wed. 102,983 off 355 from Tues.
Sugar No. 11 spot 20.93

SUGAR, Domestic (NYCSE)—112,000 lb.; ¢ per lb.

Season High	Season Low	Month	High	Low	Close	Chg.	Open Int.
22.51	15.50	Mar	22.51	22.50	22.51	+ 0.76	574
23.65	23.50	May	23.65	23.50	24.09	+ 1.00	2018
23.95	15.55	Jul	23.80	23.80	23.95	+ 1.00	1896
21.46	16.00	Sep			24.23	+ 1.00	658
23.33	23.33	Nov			24.33	+ 1.00	221
21.26	18.46	Mar			23.93	+ 1.00	386

Est. sales 144; sales Wed. 60.
Total open interest Wed. 6,753 up 12 from Tues.
Sugar No. 12 spot 23.01

MAINE POTATOES (NYM)—50,000 lbs.; ¢ per lb.

Season High	Season Low	Month	High	Low	Close	Chg.	Open Int.
9.90	5.80	Mar	5.90	5.80	5.84		414
11.75	6.01	Apr	6.25	6.01	6.07	− 0.24	294
13.68	7.10	May	7.25	7.10	7.19	− 0.06	3402
7.00	7.75	Nov	6.99	6.85	6.99	+ 0.01	77

Est. sales 710; sales Wed. 709.
Total open interest Wed. 4,187 up 155 from Tues.

COCOA (NYCO)—30,000 lb.; ¢ per lb.

Season High	Season Low	Month	High	Low	Close	Chg.	Open Int.
174.50	122.00	Mar	145.50	143.20	144.10	− 1.90	2756
166.00	125.00	May	145.20	143.10	143.80	− 1.70	2496
162.25	127.75	Jul	145.00	142.50	143.60	− 1.90	2013
162.25	130.00	Sep	146.25	144.75	144.35	− 2.10	560
3,400	2,950	Dec	3,245	3,240	3,210	− 0.50	192
3,300	3,040				3,253	− 0.41	42

Est. sales 1,982; sales Wed. 2,965.
Total open interest Wed. 8,059 up 872 from Tues.

	INITIAL	MAINTENANCE
CHICAGO BOARD OF TRADE		
Broilers	750.00	500.00
Corn (5 M Bu.)	1000.00	650.00
Plywood	800.00	700.00
Silver (5 M Oz.)	20,000.00	15,000.00
Soybeans (5 M Bu.)	3000.00	2500.00
Soybean Meal	1500.00	1000.00
Soybean Oil	1200.00	900.00
Wheat (5 M Bu.)	1500.00	800.00
GNMA	3000.00	2500.00
T-Bonds	3000.00	2500.00
CHICAGO MERCANTILE EXCHANGE		
Pork Bellies	1750.00	1250.00
Live Cattle	1500.00	1000.00
Eggs	700.00	500.00
Hogs	1000.00	700.00
Lumber	1000.00	700.00
Potatoes, Idaho	500.00	300.00
INTERNATIONAL MONETARY MARKET		
T-Bills	3000.00	2500.00
IMM Gold	9000.00	7500.00
D-Marks	5500.00	4500.00
S-Francs	5500.00	4500.00
Yen	4000.00	3500.00
B-Pound	4000.00	3500.00
C-Dollar	2000.00	1500.00
NEW YORK MARKETS		
Cocoa	2000.00	1500.00
Coffee	4500.00	3000.00
Copper	3000.00	2500.00
Cotton	1200.00	800.00
Orange Juice	1750.00	1400.00
Platinum	3000.00	2500.00
Potatoes, Maine	500.00	300.00
Silver (5 M Oz.)	10,000.00	7,500.00
Sugar (No. 11)	2000.00	1750.00
MIDAMERICA COMMODITY EXCHANGE		
Cattle	750.00	600.00
Soybeans (1 M Bu.)	600.00	500.00
Corn (1 M Bu.)	200.00	140.00
Hogs (15 M Lbs.)	600.00	500.00
Oats (5 M Bu.)	400.00	300.00
Silver (1 M Oz.)	4000.00	3000.00
Wheat (1 M Bu.)	300.00	220.00
Gold	3000.00	2250.00

Author's note: Initial margin is the minimum deposit required to purchase one contract. Maintenance margin is the minimum margin that must stay in the account, e.g., a speculator deposits $750 and buys one broiler contract. If the price of broilers falls to the point that he loses over $250 and therefore there is less than $500 left in the account he must deposit more money or be sold out.

Gold as an Investment

In 1966 in my first book, *Anyone Can Make a Million*, I wrote that gold which was then $35 per ounce, would go up to at least $100 per ounce. In 1971 when gold had reached $80, I raised my prediction to $200. By 1979 I said, in the first edition of this book, that "it is fairly obvious that much higher prices are coming: $250 within the year, $500 or even $1,000 within five years."

Well one year has gone by and gold has soared to over $600 an ounce! What now? I believe that this is just the beginning and we are obviously already well on our way to the $1,000 I predicted, although it obviously won't go straight up and there will be large, intermediate swings.

The logic is inescapable. Firstly, we should be aware that gold has not really gone up in price by a single penny, that is a real penny. If you turn one ounce of gold into U.S. dollars, it will buy almost exactly the same amount of goods in the supermarket that one ounce of gold bought seven years back. No, gold has not gone up at all; it is the dollar that has gone down! And the reason the dollar has gone down in value is that there are twice as many of them

71

as there were seven years ago. Its just as though you were slicing a pie. If you cut it into four pieces they are all large and filling. But if you make eight slices out of that same pie, they are only half as big and half as filling. Yet in both cases they are a "slice" albeit representing very different amounts. It's just the same with the dollar. Today's dollar is called the same but it represents far less than the dollar of yesteryear.

So the question we must pose is not how high will gold go, but rather how low will the dollar sink. There is no bottom nor is there any point at which gold will stop rising. People tend to think there is some magic number, so they ask me, "What is gold worth?" when they should be asking, "What is gold worth today?" You wouldn't ask, "What is an apple worth?" Everyone understands that apples will cost more next year because of inflation. Gold is a commodity just like apples and it too will cost more next year.

Gold has one special quality that other commodities do not. It can be stored forever without deterioration and because it is rare, a small amount represents a lot of value. And this is the reason that since the beginning of recorded history nations have used gold as an international medium of exchange. It is just a way to make trading easier. If there was no international trading medium, how could one nation exchange its wheat for another's oil, its cars for another's potatoes. Trade would slow to a crawl. Every transaction would have to be done by barter with endless haggling. How much quicker when we know that fifty pounds of apples are worth one ounce of gold and so is one pair of shoes.

But since 1932 and Maynard Keynes, gold is not used as a medium of exchange. Instead nations pay for other nations goods with IOUs which they call dollars or yen or marks and those IOUs are worth more or worth less depending on how rapidly they are pumped out. The United States and Canada have both issued far too many IOUs in relation to their assets and as time goes by those IOUs look less and less attractive to the people who are trading goods for them. The world needs some acceptable *constant* medium of exchange of which the value does not depend on the policies of any government and which cannot become worthless if a government changes.

That medium need not be gold. It could be silver or wampum or sheep skins or platinum, but it must be indefinitely storeable without losing its qualities. Its total world supply must either remain constant or else grow at a pre-determined rate. And it is these requirements that eliminate everything but gold. We can't use sheepskins because it would be too easy for someone to breed zillions of sheep (and anyway they smell). We can't use wampum because it gradually deteriorates. We can't use silver because there is so much of it in the world that huge quantities would have to be transported with every inter-governmental fiscal transaction. We can't use platinum because there isn't enough of it. There is no magic in gold, but it *is* the only suitable medium of exchange.

And that brings into proper focus the comment emanating from the U.S. Department of the Treasury in August 1978 when that body increased its monthly gold sales from 300,000 ounces to 600,000 ounces. The spokesman said, "We're doing this to protect the U.S. dollar and to hurry up the demonetization of gold." What the Treasury was really doing was demonetizing the dollar, not the gold. It makes one wonder whether the gentlemen running that Department are villains or are just plain stupid.

Many nations in the past have gotten themselves into a

financial bind through overspending and have attempted to solve that problem by abandoning gold and using paper money or IOUs. (The Romans substituted silver for gold and then brass for silver.) Invariably, the same result ensues. As the citizenry and other nations are flooded with paper money, there is a rush to get rid of this paper, which has no constant value, by buying hard goods including gold. Some countries attempt to prevent this by forbidding their own nationals from owning gold. All that happens, in that case, is that other things, such as jewellery or antiques, are purchased in its place. And that in turn produces inflation, as more and more paper money is spent on an increasingly scarce supply of hard goods.

Inflations all end the same way with a cataclysmic flood of worthless paper money which finally no one will accept. A new currency must then be created and in order to restore confidence, it must be backed with something tangible, and you can be sure that something won't be sheepskins.

So back to gold. Certainly, it should be bought as an inflation hedge just like any other store of real value. But gold is an especially good buy because sooner or later the United States is going to have to return to it as a medium of exchange. The later that day comes, the higher the price that gold will bring. $600 per ounce sounds like a lot today; $2,500 per ounce is inevitable if present economic policies are continued. And that won't sound so ridiculous if you realize the $2,500 ounce of gold will buy only the same amount of goods it buys today. In my lifetime, I've seen that very thing happen in Germany, in China, in Uruguay, and in Chile. Why should America be immune from the simple law of economics that says that if you spend more than you earn, people won't want your IOUs.

Let me stress however that gold is not going to go straight up. Unquestionably, there will be intermediate dips which will frighten out the weak holders as interest rates continue to rise, but high interest rates produce high unemployment and recession and these rates will surely have to be lowered before the 1980 U.S. elections if the Democrats are to have a chance. So we will see a new surge in gold and even higher record prices in 1980.

Gold Bars

Gold bars are the cheapest way to buy gold. The bars are pure and cost only the quoted value of their gold content on the day of purchase. However, this is really not a very practical way to invest in gold because the bars are heavy, there is always the danger of their being stolen, they must be insured and they can only be resold at the same place you bought them (or else they must be reassayed). There are other problems. One veteran New York open-line radio host put his life savings into gold bars and ruptured himself when carrying them to a safety deposit vault! I don't recommend gold bars.

Gold Coins and Wafers

Buying ancient gold coins has been a very profitable hobby in recent years, but here, too, many extraneous factors intrude, including the rarity of the coins, the popularity of that particular country's coins, and the condition of the piece so that actual gold content of the coin may not be the major factor in its value. In addition, coins of this type sell for anywhere from 25 to 1,000 times the value of the actual gold content in the item. An upward move in the price of gold is not necessarily reflected in the value of the coins. Buying old coins is an excellent inflation hedge, but it is not the best way to invest in gold.

With one exception, modern gold coins are worse than

ancient coins as an investment. Many nations now find it profitable to mint so-called proof gold coins at premium prices. A typical example was the $100 18-carat Olympic gold coin issued by Canada in 1976. The coins were sold at $140 each in a high pressure international campaign and so many of them were produced that they had no chance of increasing in price because of rarity. They certainly couldn't go up in real value because their gold content was worth about $45. Four years after issue, with gold at an all time high, these coins were still selling at the original price. All the lovely gold commemorative coins from various Caribbean countries that are advertised periodically fall into the same boat. They are a foolish investment with no chance of profit.

The exception is the Krugerrand. This common one-ounce coin is issued by the South African Government and is sold at the value of the gold that day plus a modest 6% premium. Krugerrand are about the size of a half dollar, can be easily stored in a safety deposit vault, are handily transportable, and can be bought or sold at any bank or currency exchange anywhere in the world at that day's gold value. And if you ever have to leave in a hurry, (don't laugh—that's the reason they are so popular in Europe) a pocketfull will sustain you for a long time. Everybody should have a few Krugerrand but this is not the best place for large gold investments.

Similar to the Krugerrand is Canada's Maple Leaf coin which also contains one ounce of gold and sells at about 8% above gold's value on the day of sale. However, a major drawback to both the Maple Leaf and the Krugerrand is the fact that in most provinces these coins are subject to sales tax. Gold wafers are *not* subject to sales tax and for this reason are a better buy for large amounts of money. Wafers can be purchased in one-, two-, five- or ten-ounce sizes and sell for the net value of gold that day. The best place to buy them is the Bank of Nova Scotia.

Gold Certificates

One of the best ways to buy gold is through the medium of a certificate — a piece of paper certifying that you own *x* ounces of gold. Such certificates are sold in any amount by the Bank of Nova Scotia and cost the price of gold that day plus a very small charge for storage. The advantage of certificates over bullion is that there is no risk of theft and if you should lose the certificate all that is required to collect your gold is to swear an affidavit and deposit a bond which will cost twenty-five dollars.

Gold certificates are a great way to invest in gold.

Gold Stocks

What about gold stocks? Gold stocks can be a very good investment, but many of these stocks will profit only the promoter behind them. These are the mining prospects, selling for pennies or for a few dollars, which are looking for an ore body or which have a low grade ore but are "waiting for higher prices". In other words, just because a company calls itself a gold mine doesn't make it so and it's a pretty good rule of thumb to eliminate all of these by simply asking the size of the company's dividend. If it's producing gold and making money it will be paying a dividend and if there is no dividend, it is probably not a good buy.

One thing for sure, if a broker phones long distance to promote a gold stock, run for the hills. He's not doing it because he likes you. It's hard to believe, but thousands of people still lose millions of dollars this way every year.

There are however good investments in gold stocks. In last year's first edition of this book I pointed out that the major decision must be whether to buy North American or South African gold stocks. My analysis at that time showed that the South African companies were by far the best buy both as to size of dividends and equity behind each dollar of share value. The great risk of course was political unrest and for that reason I favoured the North American gold mines.

That having been said I pointed out the best investments in South African golds, and looking back I find it hard to believe how well these companies have done.

Name	Price (Oct. 30/78)	Recent Price (Jan. 28/80)
East Driefontein	$ 9.75	$25
Hartesbeestfontein	16.50	58
Randfontein	45.00	67
Western Deep Levels	11.25	38
Southvaal	7.20	22
Bracken	.90	4
Stilfontein	4.35	15
Welkom	4.25	13

Wow! It is my belief that these 1980 prices fairly reflect the value of those gold mines considering the political risks involved and I would advise my readers to take profits by selling those stocks and switching into the big three North American golds which have not moved up nearly as much in price. These are Dome Mines, Campbell Red Lake, and Home Stake Mines, all of which are listed on the New York Stock Exchange. Dome and Campbell Red Lake are also listed on the Toronto Stock Exchange.

Dome Mines was trading at $83 when the first edition of this book came out last year. Since then the stock has been split two for one and as of January 1980 was trading around $50, so that it had not moved up nearly as much as it should considering the increase in gold's price. In addition to its own gold mine in Ontario, it owns large oil holdings through Dome Petroleum, 56% of Campbell Red Lake, 60% of Sigma Mines, plus various holdings in Denison Mines, Canada Tungsten, Mattagami Lake and Panarctic Oil. Dome is the conglomerate of the natural resources field.

Dome has twelve million shares outstanding and earns about three dollars per share, out of which one dollar is paid in dividends. It is hard to evaluate Dome because of its huge oil holdings, but the company's net asset value is certainly equal to its trading price, and its potential is virtually unlimited.

Campbell Red Lake is not only a subsidiary of Dome; it is intimately involved in its parent company's affairs, holding interests in Dome Petroleum, Panarctic Oils and Denison Mines. The company will earn about one dollar per share in 1980, out of which half is paid in dividends. When I recommended the stock last year it was trading at $31. It has since split two for one and by January 1980 it was back up over $31.

Homestake is the richest gold mine in the United

States, with diversified interests in lead, zinc, silver and uranium. In the late seventies, the company did well, chiefly from its huge uranium holdings, while gold meant less and less to its earnings. The company's vast deposits of "wealth in the ground" also include base metals. As of January 1980 it was earning about $2.50 per share and paid out half of that in dividends. When I recommended it in 1979 it was quoted around $35 and one year later it was over $50.

At current prices I do not think there is any question that Dome is the best all-round buy, but all three continue to look cheap.

Gold Bonds

There is another excellent way to invest in gold, through the medium of gold bonds which trade on the Paris Bourse. These are called Giscard d'Estaing bonds after the French president and their price will vary depending on the value of gold as they are convertible into that metal. As I write this in early 1980, the most popular issue is the 7% of January 16, 1988 which trades at 5380 francs. Although these bonds are a great way to buy gold they have the disadvantage of trading only in France and it is difficult to buy them in Canada as only one or two brokers will call a market. (A similarly exciting but difficult to trade bond is the Petro bond based on the price of oil. These bonds trade on the Mexican exchange — the most popular issue is the 12⅝% of 1982 trading at 125 pesos.)

Investors in these bonds have done very well. The 7% French gold bonds which were issued in 1973 have already moved up 5½ times and all the gold bonds have doubled in the past year. The current Mexican Oil Bonds give a yield of 10% and run for three years and as the price of crude oil increases the maturity value of the bond increases accordingly.

Gold on the Future Exchanges

Finally we come to the most desirable way to invest or speculate in gold: by buying bullion on the future exchanges. Gold is listed on three exchanges, Chicago Mercantile, New York's Monetary, and Winnipeg. The contracts traded in New York and Chicago are for 100 ounces and those in Winnipeg for 100 or 400 ounces. In Winnipeg, there is a slight advantage in commission, but the market is much thinner and therefore less liquid. Here are the trading results for one day. The volume in Winnipeg was only one contract while 9,000 traded in Chicago and 24,000 in New York.

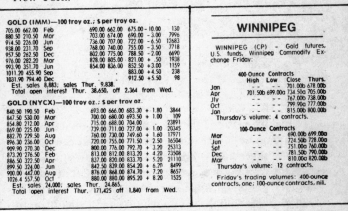

GOLD (IMM)—100 troy oz.; $ per troy oz.

			High	Low	Close	Chg.	Open Int.
705.00	662.00	Feb	690.00	662.00	675.00	-10.00	130
880.50	210.50	Mar	703.00	674.00	690.00	-3.00	7996
914.50	226.00	Jun	736.00	707.00	722.00	-6.50	12683
938.00	231.70	Sep	768.00	740.00	755.00	-3.50	7718
957.50	262.50	Dec	802.00	775.00	788.50	-2.00	6690
976.00	282.20	Mar	828.00	805.00	821.00	+.50	1938
993.90	351.70	Jun	854.00	836.00	852.50	+3.00	1159
1011.20	455.90	Sep			883.00	+4.50	238
1031.90	794.40	Dec			912.50	+5.50	98

Est. sales 8,883; sales Thur. 9,838.
Total open interest Thur. 38,650, off 2,364 from Wed.

GOLD (NYCX)—100 troy oz.; $ per troy oz.

			High	Low	Close	Chg.	Open Int.
840.50	190.50	Feb	693.00	666.00	683.30	+1.80	3844
847.50	530.00	Mar	700.00	680.00	693.50	+1.00	109
854.80	212.00	Apr	715.00	688.00	704.00		23891
869.00	225.00	Jun	739.00	711.00	727.00	+1.00	20345
882.70	229.50	Aug	760.00	730.00	749.60	+1.60	17971
896.30	236.00	Oct	720.00	755.00	771.50	+2.50	16504
909.90	270.30	Dec	800.00	776.00	792.70	+3.20	25313
873.20	276.50	Feb	813.00	812.00	813.20	+4.20	23508
886.50	322.50	Apr	837.00	820.00	833.70	+5.20	21110
899.50	324.00	Jun	842.50	839.00	854.20	+6.20	8499
900.00	442.00	Aug	876.00	868.00	874.70	+7.20	8657
1026.4	557.50	Oct	880.00	880.00	895.20	+8.20	1525

Est. sales 24,000; sales Thur. 24,865.
Total open interest Thur. 171,425 off 1,840 from Wed.

WINNIPEG

WINNIPEG (CP) - Gold futures, U.S. funds, Winnipeg Commodity Exchange Friday:

400-Ounce Contracts

	High	Low	Close	Thurs.
Jan	--	--	701.00b	678.00b
Apr	701.50b	699.00a	734.50a	705.00b
Jly	--	--	767.00b	738.00b
Oct	--	--	799.90a	777.00b
Jan	--	--	815.00b	800.00b

Thursday's volume: 4 contracts.

100-Ounce Contracts

	High	Low	Close	Thurs.
Mar	--	--	690.00b	699.00a
Jun	--	--	724.50b	728.00a
Spt	--	--	751.00b	760.00b
Dec	--	--	781.50b	790.00b
Mar	--	--	810.00a	820.00b

Thursday's volume: 12 contracts.

Friday's trading volumes: 400-ounce contracts, one; 100-ounce contracts, nil.

Gold Listing from The Globe and Mail

Because of the much greater volume, the difference between the bid and ask is smaller on the two U.S. exchanges, and so it's easier both to buy and to sell. Therefore, it is wiser to use Chicago or New York rather than Winnipeg.

Note that the gold sells by delivery date and the further away the delivery chosen, the higher the price. This is only partially because the market expects a rise in the price of gold. The difference between the futures price for October 1980 of $755 and October 1981 of $895.20 also represents the interest on the invested money plus storage charges for one year.

The advantages of buying gold in this way are:

(1) No risk of theft. The buyer never actually takes delivery of the gold.
(2) No insurance costs.
(3) Low margin. The down payment on one contract of 100 ounces worth about $70,000 is only $8,000. This provides big leverage.
(4) Price changes depend only on the value of the gold, eliminating extraneous factors such as size of ore body or labour unrest.
(5) Large profits can be made very quickly through the use of pyramiding. My trade sheet for August 1979, which appears opposite, is an example of this type of pyramiding.

Note that between June 27 and July 17 I set the base of the pyramid by buying four gold contracts between $293.40 and $309. I then built my pyramid by buying two more contracts the next day between $312 and $314 and continued to build the pyramid till the end of August paying as high as $326.20. Thus with the pyramid built I had a $18,030 profit with gold at $326.70 and all this took place within a period of eight weeks.

Of course gold does fluctuate and I was lucky in my timing, but the overall trend is up because of inflation. Provided you don't get in over your head and can ride out short term reversals, you will make money. If your capital is limited, it is advisable to protect gold positions with stops $20 below the current price. This limits any loss and you can always reinstate your position when the downward surge

DATE	BOUGHT	SOLD	COMMODITY	TRADE PRICE	SETTLEMENT PRICE	DEBIT	CREDIT
			BEGINNING LEDGER BALANCE			12,431.13	21,256.70
79/08/03	C$25000 REC						30.00
79/08/06		2	79DEC GOLD N3				
79/08/13	C$10000.00		DISB			4,542.63	
79/08/15	5	5	79OCT HOGS N3				1,005.00
79/08/22	1		79DEC JAP.YEN C2			1,942.50	
79/08/24	2		79DEC JAP.YEN-C2			3,660.00	
79/08/29	C$15000 DISB					12,815.04	
79/08/30	2		2 79DEC GOLD N3				7,410.00
79/08/31	1		79DEC GOLD N3				220.00
79/08/31		2	79NOV O.JUICE N4			620.00	
**** OPEN TRADES FOLLOW ****							
79/08/03		2	79DEC CDN DLR C2	84.96	85.82	1,720.00	
79/08/07		1	79DEC CDN DLR C2	85.14	85.82	680.00	
79/08/07		1	79DEC CDN DLR C2	85.25	85.82	590.00	
		4				2,990.00	
79/06/27	1		79DEC GOLD N3	293.40	326.70		3,330.00
79/07/06	1		79DEC GOLD N3	302.50	326.70		2,440.00
79/07/16	1		79DEC GOLD N3	307.50	326.70		1,920.00
79/07/17	1		79DEC GOLD N3	309.00	326.70		1,770.00
79/07/18	1		79DEC GOLD N3	312.20	326.70		1,450.00
79/07/18	1		79DEC GOLD N5	314.30	326.70		1,240.00
79/08/10	1		79DEC GOLD N3	311.60	326.70		1,510.00
79/08/15	1		79DEC GOLD N3	308.50	326.70		1,840.00
79/08/22	1		79DEC GOLD N3	319.10	326.70		760.00
79/08/22	1		79DEC GOLD N3	321.20	326.70		550.00
79/08/23	1		79DEC GOLD C3	321.40	326.70		530.00
79/08/28	1		79DEC GOLD C3	326.20	326.70		50.00
79/08/31	2		79DEC GOLD N3	323.50	326.70		640.00
	14			OPEN TRADE EQUITY			18,030.00
				LEDGER BALANCE		10,289.60	15,040.00
MARGIN—REG							
INIT - MAINT							

stops. This is what I did in January of 1980, buying gold at $630 and seeing it move up $40 and then down to what I had originally paid. I had approached my stopping point and I sold out, but I bought it back again a few days later and waited for the next upward move.

If you don't wish to gamble but just to own gold and pay for it in full, buy the most distantly traded month and literally put it away. It doesn't make sense to use all your cash because no interest is paid. This is one place where government or other interest-bearing certificates make sense. Put down the minimum margin in gold and place the balance in short term government notes. It's just as though you had bought the gold outright but without the nuisance of looking after it. When the due date nears you just sell it out and buy a distant month in its place.

It is all common sense. Whether you believe in gold in some mystical way, as do so many of the "gold bugs" or whether you just acknowledge that everything is going up in price, in either case gold is one of the most practical ways to protect capital.

I personally do it all the sensible ways. I own Campbell Red Lake stock, I buy gold futures, and I even have a few Krugerrand, I haven't lost on any of them in the past. I expect to continue to profit in the future.

Making Money by Selling
U. S. Dollars

Suppose you already own your own home and don't want to gamble in commodities or speculate with gold. Where can you invest your money where the capital is safe and where there is some real return on it? In other words, what is today's equivalent of the government bond of pre-inflationary days?

The U.S. and Canadian dollars have been falling steadily in value for the past ten years as more and more of them have been printed, but this is not true of other currencies from countries with non-inflationary policies, such as Switzerland, Japan, West Germany and Chile. The German mark still buys almost as much hard goods as it did ten years ago and the Swiss franc buys even more. Too bad our savings are not in one of those foreign currencies.

Take care, the last time I made that suggestion a lady in Alberta actually went out and converted all her life savings into Swiss francs — actual bank notes — which she took home with her. The idea was fine and she did make money but the method was all wrong. If you do convert your dollars into other currency, it's smart to do it in a way that will give a return. Ten years ago, anyone could simply have opened a savings account in a foreign bank and happily drawn interest while the dollar sagged but so many people did that and there was such a huge inflow of U.S. currency into the hard currency countries that their own economies became threatened. Other countries responded by restricting foreign deposits and Switzerland went so far as to charge foreigners interest on their accounts instead of paying it. At first, this was nominal but when that didn't stop the inflow they imposed a penalty interest rate of 10% every ninety days!

Buying Foreign Currency Bonds

The smartest way to hold foreign currency is through Samurai bonds, bonds issued by non-Japanese governments or non-Japanese corporations but payable in Japanese yen in both principal and interest. These bonds have grown rapidly in popularity. In 1970, only 25 million dollars worth were issued while in 1977 $1.2 billion were issued. The final figure for 1978 was over 5 billion dollars. The Japanese Government has welcomed such bonds because of their desire to lower their balance of payments surplus, and foreign borrowers have made the trek to Japan because of the low interest rates. (I think they are crazy for when pay off time comes they may well find that they saved 2% in interest and lost 100% in a capital loss.) But from the buyer's point of view, Samurai bonds are a perfect vehicle with which to change weakening dollars into hard currency and to draw interest on that foreign currency.

An amazing variety of countries have used Samurai bonds to raise money and the interest rate will vary with the credit worthiness of the issuer. Here is a list of current Samurai bonds:

Name of Issue	Coupon	Date of Maturity	Amount Issue (billion yen)
No. 1 World Bank	7.75%	July 10, 1981	11
Asian Development Bank no. 3	7.3	May 6, 1982	10
Australia no. 1	6.9	July 25, 1982	10
Province of Quebec no. 1	6.9	September 28, 1984	10
Brazil no. 1	8.25	November 12, 1985	10
Finland no. 1	9.25	July 17, 1987	10
New Zealand no. 1	9.0	November 4, 1987	10
European Investment Bank no. 1	8.9	August 3, 1988	10
Denmark no. 1	9.0	November 30, 1988	10
Province of Manitoba no. 1	8.6	February 28, 1987	12
Banque Française du Commerce Exterieur	7.6	July 13, 1989	20
Ireland no. 1	7.2	August 5, 1989	16
Inter-American Development Bank	6.8	September 29, 1989	15
Province of New Brunswick	7.0	September 30, 1989	12
Spain no. 1	7.0	October 29, 1987	15
Venezuela no. 1	6.8	December 15, 1989	20
Singapore no. 2	6.7	December 27, 1987	15
Province of Manitoba no. 2	6.7	January 30, 1990	15
Korea Development Bank	6.7	January 29, 1988	10
City of Oslo	6.6	February 27, 1990	15
Finland no. 3	6.7	February 26, 1988	25
Societe Nationale des Chemins de Fer Française (SNCF)	6.6	March 10, 1990	20
Philippines	6.7	March 30, 1988	15
Malaysia	6.5	April 11, 1988	15
Argentina	6.4	April 17, 1986	15
Norway	5.7	April 18, 1983	25
RENFE (Spanish National R.R.)	6.5	April 25, 1990	16
Sweden	6.3	April 25, 1990	40
Province of Quebec no. 2	6.4	May 23, 1990	30
Republic of Venezuela no. 2	6.4	May 30, 1990	40
Eurofima	6.3	May 26, 1990	10
BNDE	6.5	May 30, 1988	16
City of Stockholm	6.4	May 15, 1990	10
Industrialization Fund of Finland	6.4	June 18, 1990	5

Sellers of Samurai bonds have already taken a fearful beating. Take as a horrible example, the province of Manitoba's issue in February 1977 of 12 billion yen worth of these bonds. At the then conversion of 226 yen to the Canadian dollar, the hapless treasurer of that province ended up receiving about 5 million dollars and assumed that he was to pay 8.6% interest per year. But because of the fall of the Canadian dollar since then, one dollar today buys only 165 yen so the Province of Manitoba which thought it was paying low interest is actually now paying almost 11% annual interest on its loan. Worse, if they were to pay that loan off today it would cost them well over $7 million dollars. Who knows how high the final bill will be by the time those bonds come due in 1987?

But it is not my purpose here to criticize stupid governments or politicians. Rather it is to show how to take advantage of their stupidity, and that is by *buying* Samurai Bonds. If you had been one of the lucky buyers of a Manitoba bond in 1977, you would have already earned 40% on your money in interest and capital gain! Of course one should use a certain amount of discrimination. I'm not at all sure that the Government of Korea will be around in 1988 to pay off their bonds and so I wouldn't buy them. But I have no doubts that Manitoba, Denmark, and Oslo are good for theirs. Buyers of these bonds receive the full interest return, for unlike other securities the Japanese Government does not hold back any withholding tax.

Where does one buy such bonds? Unlike most other securities, in the case of Samurai Bonds there are more would-be buyers than there are new Samurai bonds available, so most dealers are not anxious to sell to small investors. Two companies that will handle small purchases are Daiwa Securities in New York City and Nomura Securities in Toronto's Commerce Court.

Samurai Bonds are not the only way to invest safely in foreign currencies. Many bonds are issued denominated in German marks or Swiss francs. For example, last year the World Bank issued six-year notes paying 5.75% and ten-year notes paying 6% denominated in German marks. They are available through any international broker.

When buying German, Swiss or Japanese bonds, it is wise to purchase new issues rather than outstanding bonds already trading at a premium because with the new issue you avoid paying commission.

Trading in Foreign Currency

So much for the person playing it safe. How should a speculator gamble in foreign currency? Once again we must look to the Chicago Currency Exchange where the currencies of France, Mexico, England, Canada, Germany and Japan are traded against the U.S. dollar. A list of quotes and trades appears every day in *The Globe and Mail*:

MEXICAN PESO (IMM)—1 million pesos; $ per peso

.04337	.03445	Mar	.04326	.04324	.04325 - 09	755
.04315	.03325	Jun	.04226	.04201	.04202 + 02	1054
.04135	.03230	Sep	.04105	.04090	.04090	579
.04005	.03175	Dec	.03995	.03994	.03995	339
.03900	.03550	Mar	.03900	.03870	.03900 + 01	188
.03790	.03450	Jun	.03790	.03785	.03785 + 11	70

Est. sales 70; sales Wed. 31.
Total open interest Wed. 2,985, off 5 from Tues.

SWISS FRANC (IMM)—125,000 francs; $ per franc

.6968	.6030	Mar	.6226	.6153	.6169 - 56	7964
.7010	.6110	Jun	.6360	.6278	.6298 - 61	2482
.7210	.6455	Sep	.6470	.6378	.6420 - 63	957
.6831	.6300	Dec	.6590	.6500	.6506 - 89	77

Est. sales 3,774; sales Wed. 1,764.
Total open interest Wed. 11,480, up 369 from Tues.

BRITISH POUND (IMM)—25,000 pounds; $ per pound

2.3050	2.0000	Mar	2.2600	2.2530	2.2565 + 45	7877
2.2940	2.0620	Jun	2.2500	2.2430	2.2470 + 30	2585
2.2750	2.0450	Sep	2.2435	2.2360	2.2360 + 40	370
2.2690	2.2400	Dec			2.2300	72

Est. sales 3,308; sales Wed. 3,391.
Total open interest Wed. 10,904, off 51 from Tues.

CANADIAN DOLLAR (IMM)
100,000 dollars; $ per Canadian dollar

.8600	.8422	Mar	.8645	.8624	.8637 + 24	5648
.8725	.8445	Jun	.8665	.8645	.8657 + 21	1801
.8740	.8480	Sep	.8680	.8665	.8669 + 04	717
.8750	.8480	Dec	.8695	.8683	.8695 + 10	116
.8690	.8630	Mar			.8680	11

Est. sales 1,846; sales Wed. 1,327.
Total open interest Wed. 8,293, off 209 from Tues.

WEST GERMAN MARK (IMM)
125,000 marks; $ per mark

.6037	.5353	Mar	.5791	.5764	.5770 - 11	6954
.6050	.5385	Jun	.5878	.5847	.5858 - 21	4565
.6125	.5790	Sep	.5956	.5922	.5940 - 19	952
.6135	.6027	Dec	.6005	.5990	.6000 - 38	47

Est. sales   sales Wed. 2,048.
Total open interest Wed. 12,518, up 305 from Tues.

JAPANESE YEN (IMM)—12.5 million yen; ¢ per yen

.004890	.004052	Mar	.004219	.004209	.004217	2911
.004750	.004105	Jun	.004283	.004268	.004283 - 03	719
.004530	.004295	Sep	.004343	.004336	.004337 - 08	140
.004475	.004345	Dec			.004350	3

Est. sales 564; sales Wed. 861.
Total open interest Wed. 3,773, up 170 from Tues.

FRENCH FRANC (IMM)—250,000 francs; ¢ per franc

24700	.24590	Mar	.24700	16
25100	.25000	Jun	.25000	20

Est. sales 0; sales Wed. 0.
Total open interest Wed. 36, unchanged from Tues.

The essential point to remember is that the long-term trends of the yen, the Swiss franc and the German mark is upwards while the U.S. and the Canadian dollars are in the course of a long-term deterioration.

In currency trading, margin is even lower than with commodities, usually running about 2.5%. Thus each Canadian dollar contract represents 100,000 Canadian dollars but requires only a $2,500 down payment. This results in rapid profits and losses. For example if you had sold one Canadian dollar contract the day after René Lévesque was elected Premier of Quebec, you would have seen your $2,500 grow to $12,500 within one year without pyramiding and to over $200,000 with pyramiding. This was because the dollar went straight down. Pyramiding is dangerous, however, because currencies usually have zigs and zags in their moves and with such a tiny down payment you should leave yourself some room.

An example of how to sell a collapsing currency on its way down appears opposite.

And don't let anyone tell you that selling U.S. or Canadian dollars is unpatriotic or that speculation is the cause of the collapse. It just isn't true. Every speculator ends up buying and selling exactly the same number of dollars. If I sell short one million Canadian dollars today, I must buy back exactly the same amount of dollars before my contract comes due in six months. My final total effect on the level of the dollar is zero. The real cause of our currency's collapse is the terrible overspending by our politicians. Being human, they will blame anyone before admitting their own culpability. Thus I was amazed one day when sitting in Ontario's legislature to be suddenly singled out by the leader of the Liberal Party who said that the real cause of high food prices were people like me because I traded in the commodity futures market!

DATE	BOUGHT	SOLD	COMMODITY	TRADE PRICE	SETTLEMENT PRICE	DEBIT	CREDIT
**** O P E N		T R A	D E S F O L L O	W ****			
77-09-29		2	BEGINNING LEDGER BALANCE			2,751.78	
77-10-03		1	78MAR CAN-DOLLAR	93.00	90.18		5,640.00
77-10-03		1	78MAR CAN-DOLLAR	92.51	90.18		2,330.00
77-10-03		1	78MAR CAN-DOLLAR	92.62	90.18		2,440.00
77-10-04		1	78MAR CAN-DOLLAR	92.65	90.18		2,470.00
77-10-04		1	78MAR CAN-DOLLAR	92.20	90.18		2,020.00
77-10-05		1	78MAR CAN-DOLLAR	92.30	90.18		2,120.00
77-10-05		1	78MAR CAN-DOLLAR	92.06	90.18		1,880.00
77-10-06		1	78MAR CAN-DOLLAR	92.24	90.18		2,060.00
77-10-06		1	78MAR CAN-DOLLAR	91.75	90.18		1,570.00
77-10-11		1	78MAR CAN-DOLLAR	91.85	90.18		1,670.00
77-10-11		1	78MAR CAN-DOLLAR	91.63	90.18		1,450.00
77-10-11		1	78MAR CAN-DOLLAR	91.66	90.18		1,480.00
77-10-12		1	78MAR CAN-DOLLAR	91.48	90.18		1,300.00
77-10-13		1	78MAR CAN-DOLLAR	90.85	90.18		670.00
77-10-24		1	78MAR CAN-DOLLAR	89.61	90.18	570.00	
		16					28,530.00*
			OPEN TRADE EQUITY				28,530.00

MARGIN——REQ
INIT   MAINT
40000 32000

Perhaps not surprisingly, the accusation came from a gentleman who had advocated huge welfare and farm support programs and whose party has led my country to its present state of near insolvency. I didn't take the accusation too seriously — nor did anyone else — but such attacks make great newspaper headlines. And it doesn't really matter whether they are true or not. If they reach the press, enough people will believe them to make it worthwhile. So my advice is to ignore such nonsense. But if you have a thin skin, keep your trading to yourself.

The mechanics of trading currencies is exactly the same as that of trading eggs or gold. But the one great advantage is that there are far fewer factors affecting any price change. Unlike ordinary commodities, once a currency enters a trend it is rare indeed for it to reverse itself. Thus, the Canadian dollar has been steadily working its way lower since November 1976 while the U.S. dollar has been in its downtrend now for over seven years. Traders who have steadily sold these currencies short have made money year after year. But not day after day. Even the Canadian dollar in its precipitous collapse of 1977 and 1978 had brief periods of steadiness and occasionally even moved up fractionally.

So this brings me to the one danger in currency trading. Even long term trends are interrupted occasionally and on only 2½% margin this can be disastrous. So keep a reserve and don't put all your eggs in this one basket. Also this is one place where it's sensible to protect yourself with stops no more than 1% from the current market.

But despite this one caveat, currency trading is the easiest and quickest place to make big money today. The easiest and safest are Samurai or German bonds.

The essential question is what is the dollar worth? The first answer is that it is probably worth just about what it is now trading at, *but* that next year it will be worth less. Both Canada and the United States are committed to deficit financing which means pumping out more and more dollars. In 1973 a U.S. dollar would buy four German marks. Six years later it bought two German marks, and by 1982 it will probably buy only one mark. In 1989, it may take four U.S. dollars to buy one mark. Similarly with the Canadian dollar. Canada's leading economists said it wouldn't break 90¢ U.S. As I write, it is just above 86¢. So long as we continue to follow our present economic policies, the Canadian dollar will continue to deteriorate. I can easily see 80¢ in 1981 and 50¢ in 1983. And people who don't protect themselves against an improvident government are improvident investors.

Offshore Funds: How to Make Money & Minimize Taxes

The only serious drawback to investing in Samurai bonds is the fact that our government grabs a big hunk of the interest paid on these bonds. Since no one likes to pay unnecessary income tax, a strategy has been developed which avoids paying this tax. It is very simple and is done through an offshore fund. *It is perfectly legal.*

A large number of these funds have been set up by reputable foreign brokers, and a few by some not so reputable (more about that later), which will take money from U.S. and Canadian investors and with it buy hard currency bonds or stocks. The reason no income tax is payable is that the funds do not pay the interest to the investor; but instead the interest is allowed to accumulate. This defers the tax indefinitely and when the investor finally sells his shares, he pays tax only at the much lower capital gains rate.

In addition, there are ways that an investor can actually draw this interest, but still only pay tax at the lower capital gains rate. This is done by selling 10% of the holdings every year. Suppose an investor puts $50,000 into an offshore fund earning 10% a year. Normally, he would pay income tax on the $5,000 interest, leaving him with $2,500 if he were in the 50% bracket. Instead he draws no interest and in its place he sells 10% of his stock at the end of each year, giving him $5,500 in hand. He only pays a capital gains tax on this leaving him $3,900. Neat, is it not?

The only real problem with offshore funds is that they are not under the scrutiny of the SEC and so great care must be taken in choosing a reliable fund. Martonmere Securities of Toronto has prepared a list of offshore funds with well established sponsorship and financing, through which a prudent investor can place his money in hard currencies. The following pages provide a selection from their choices.

1. Fixed Income Funds

Rentak Fonds

THE FUND INVESTS IN:
The Rentak Fonds invests in German government bonds, high-quality corporate bonds, and other types of bonds.

CURRENCY DENOMINATION:
German mark (DM)

INCORPORATION AND LOCATION:
The Rentak Fonds is incorporated under the laws of the West German Republic and maintains its offices in Munich, West Germany.

SPONSORS AND ADVISORS:
Investment Advisor   Münchner Kapitalanlage AG, Munich

Banker and Custodian	Allgemeine Deutsche Credit-Anstalt
Registrar and Transfer Agent	Allgemeine Deutsche Credit-Anstalt (ADCA) Frankfurt
Auditors	Treuarbeit AG, Munich

INTEREST:

The rate of interest on German government bonds and high-quality corporate bonds varies depending on German rates. At time of writing, it is around 6%.

DIVIDENDS AND APPROPRIATION OF PROFITS:

Interest and all other income are re-invested rather than paid out; hence no dividends are paid.

TAX POSITION:

There is no withholding tax paid or withheld on interest on any of the debt securities in which the fund invests, and the fund is not subject to capital gains tax.

FUND SIZE:

At the end of June 1979 the total assets of the fund were 58 million DM, or 38 million dollars in Canadian funds.

RECORD (FINANCIAL YEAR DECEMBER 31):

	Accumulated Value DM	% Gain	Accumulated Value $ Cdn.	% Gain
May 1973	50.00	--	17.05	--
Dec. 1973	53.80	7.6	19.82	16.25
Dec. 1974	58.50	7.4	24.08	21.40
Dec. 1975	67.74	15.8	26.28	9.14
Dec. 1976	75.38	11.3	32.24	22.65
Sept. 1977	82.65	9.6	38.39	19.00
June 1979	85.02	13.4*	57.84	53.00*
Average Annual Compound Gain		11.8		24

* 18 months

Europe Obligations

THE FUND INVESTS IN:

Europe Obligations invests in high-quality government, provincial, and corporate bonds which are, with a few exceptions, not subject to withholding taxes. Basically, these are international bonds denominated in various hard currencies. The objective of the fund is capital appreciation and income.

CURRENCY DENOMINATION:
Luxembourg franc (F. Lux.)

INCORPORATION AND LOCATION:
The fund was incorporated in March, 1973 under Luxembourg law and maintains its offices in Luxembourg.

SPONSORS AND ADVISORS:

Investment Advisors	Caisse des Depots et Consignations, Banque de L'Union Europeenne, Caisse d'Epargne de l'Etat du Grand Duche de Luxembourg, Banque Generale du Phenix, US Trust Paris, Deutsche Girozentrale — Deutsche Kommunalbank.
Bankers	Caisse des Depots et Consignations, Banque de l'Union Europeene, Caisse d'Epargne de l'Etat du Grand Duche de Luxembourg.
Registrar Custodian and Transfer Agent	Caisse d'Epargne de l'Etat due Grand Duche de Luxembourg

INTEREST:
The rate of interest paid on the fund depends on the level of interest rates prevailing in the countries in which the fund invests. As of June 30, 1979, the rate of return was approximately 4.16% free of tax. At the shareholder's option, interest may be kept in the fund and compounded rather than paid out.

Except for shareholders domiciled or resident in Luxembourg, there is, at present, no Luxembourg income tax or capital gains tax payable by the fund or its shareholders.

FUND SIZE:
As of June 30, 1979, the total net assets of Europe Obligations were close to F. Lux. 417 million or 15 million (Cdn.).

VALUATION AND REDEMPTION:
The fund is valued every day and the net asset value per share is published in the *International Herald Tribune*. Payments for shares being redeemed are made in Luxembourg francs as soon as possible after valuation day.

RECORD:

	Accumulated Value F. Lux	% Gain (% Loss)	Total Value $ Cdn.	% Gain (% Loss)
April 1973	1,000.0	--	24.87	--
Dec. 1973	1,011.8	1.18	24.40	(1.89)
Dec. 1974	938.6	(7.23)	25.71	5.37
Dec. 1975	1,163.4	23.95	29.91	16.34
Dec. 1976	1,224.3	5.23	34.39	14.98
Sept. 1977	1,337.6	9.25	40.16	16.78
June 1979	1,147.0	(13.00)*	56.05	40.*
Average Annual Compound Gain		2.3		18.5

* 18 months

2. Equity Funds

Fleming Japan Fund S.A.

THE FUND INVESTS IN:
The Fleming Japan Fund invests in Japanese equities. Its main investment objective is capital appreciation and consequently only a small dividend is paid out.

CURRENCY DENOMINATION:
U.S. dollar ($U.S.)

INCORPORATION:

The fund is incorporated under the laws of the Grand Duchy of Luxembourg.

SPONSORS AND ADVISORS:

Investment Advisor	Robert Fleming Investment Management Ltd., London
Banker and Custodian	Kredietbank S.A., Luxembourgeoise, Luxembourg
Registrar and Transfer Agent	Kredeitbank S.A., Luxembourgeoise, Luxembourg
Auditors	Wimmey, Murray, Ernst & Ernst

TAX POSITION:

Under present legislation, the fund's investment income from sources within Japan is subject to normal Japanese withholding tax. No capital gains tax is payable by the fund on the realized capital appreciation of its assets. There is at present no Luxembourg income tax, withholding tax, capital gains tax, estate or inheritance tax payable by the fund or its shareholders, except for shareholders domiciled, resident or having a permanent establishment in Luxembourg. The fund is subject in Luxembourg to annual duty of 0.16% on the aggregate value of the outstanding shares of the fund. This value is calculated by reference to the Luxembourg Stock Exchange value of the shares during the preceding year. The fund is also liable to a contribution duty of 1% of the nominal value and premium on new issue of capital.

DISTRIBUTION POLICY:

Since the main objective of the fund is capital appreciation, it only pays out a small dividend.

VALUATION AND REDEMPTION:

The fund is valued weekly and the net asset value per share is published in *The Financial Times*. The shares are quoted on the Luxembourg Stock Exchange. Payment is made in U.S. dollars within the first 15 business days in which certificates are received by the fund.

FUND SIZE:

Total net assets at June 30, 1979 were 51 million dollars (U.S.)

RECORD (FINANCIAL YEAR DECEMBER 31):

	Accumulated Value $ U.S.	% Gain (% Loss)	Distribution U.S. $	Accumulated Value $ U.S.	% Gain (% Loss)
Dec. 1971	15.17	--	--	15.17	--
June 1972	22.70	49.6	--	22.47	48.1
June 1973	17.35	(23.5)	0.090	17.28	(23.0)
June 1974	19.01	10.0	0.100	18.47	6.9
June 1975	21.42	12.7	0.140	21.91	18.0
June 1976	29.45	37.4	0.125	28.53	30.0
Sept. 1977	36.76	24.8	0.150	39.44	38.2
June 1979	48.65	33.	6.375	48.15	25*
Average Annual Compound Gain		18.5			19.2
* 18 months					

In summation, offshore funds are a highly sophisticated way of protecting capital by putting it in German marks, Swiss francs, or Japanese yen while simultaneously earning a reasonable income and, most extraordinarily, shielding that income from taxation. It's a great way to invest!

What About the Stock Market?

Unlike the bond market (yecch) or the gold market (hurrah) there is no simple answer as to the future of common stocks. The reason is that because every stock represents ownership in a different company and every company faces different prospects during inflation, great discrimination is necessary.

It is fairly certain that utilities and other regulated companies will do badly in inflationary times. This is because as inflation and costs of doing business speed up, companies in this class have great difficulty in getting approval of rate increases quickly enough. Let me give one example from my own experience. When I was an MPP and inflation was running at about 6% per year, the Bell Telephone Company was faced with tremendous cost increases for both labour and materials such as copper which had sold five years earlier at 40¢ per pound and which had now reached 80¢. Yet when the Bell applied for a 6% rate increase dozens of well-meaning or popularity seeking politicians presented briefs to the regulatory body as to why the raise should not be allowed (I weep with embarrassment — I was one of them) giving as their major reason Bell's profits of millions of dollars per year. Last year I made the mistake of trying to reason with one of my former colleagues on this subject, but his response was right to the point, "Shit on return on capital and the same for the Bell Telephone Co. There aren't any votes there."

Ultimately the company did get its raise, but the hearing with all its briefs resulted in a delay of six months between initial application and final approval. It didn't matter too much in 1970, but today costs would be so much higher in six months that a new application for a raise would be needed immediately. *In inflationary times, telephone stocks and power companies are a losing proposition.*

Service companies are just about as bad because their costs go up with the inflationary rate, but there is great resistance to raising service prices at the retail level. To take the simplest example, if the cost of a haircut is raised from $3 to $6, people get fewer haircuts (or cut their own). *Service companies are a bad investment in inflationary times.*

High profile manufacturing companies are not much better. General Motors sets their price once a year and has great difficulty in putting on hefty rises even then because of governmental pressure "to set an example". I wouldn't buy manufacturing stocks today.

Well what stocks are worth buying? Only those that are inflation proof and there aren't many of those. An inflation proof stock is one that has "wealth in the ground", that is not susceptible to government control. All wealth in the ground stocks are not inflation proof and this has been illustrated only too well in Canada and the United States in recent years. When world oil and gas prices surged in the mid-seventies, Canada passed laws forcing the oil companies to sell their oil to Canadians at prices far below the world market price. Canadian voters applauded and since there are far more of them than there are shareholders in Imperial Oil, the Government continued this policy. Similarly the U.S. Government behaved equally short sightedly by putting a ceiling on gas prices — short sighted because any such artificial ceiling automatically reduces exploration.

So the only stocks worth buying today are those with wealth in the ground where there is no advantage to the government to jump in. That includes companies exporting their product (like the Canadian lumber companies) for no politician cares what prices are like in another country, companies producing something that is not considered a necessity (gold mines fall into this category), and companies holding big land spreads. These few stocks will move up in price at least as fast as the dollar loses its buying power, but they are the only group that will do so. Other individual stocks may do well, for example a drug company making a major discovery or a manufacturing concern that is attractive as a takeover, but in general most stocks are not inflation protected and should be avoided.

One extra dividend to wealth-in-the-ground stocks is that they are a special attraction for take-over offers from nervous holders of cash seeking good investment. Asbestos Corporation was an excellent example of this type of investment. In the fall of 1977, the company had enormous deposits of asbestos in Quebec, had a break-up value of $65 per share, paid an 8% dividend, and was trading at $23. I bought a total of 5,000 shares for myself, and attempted to persuade all my friends it was the buy of the age. I even wrote an article in October 1977 for the *Magazine of Wall Street* saying that it was a sure way to make money. I never

did find anyone else who bought the stock, but only thirty days later the Quebec Government made an offer to buy out the company. I made a killing! One of my trade slips is shown above.

As for preferred stocks, none should ever be bought. In a preferred, the holder sacrifices participation in profits in return for a steady dividend and that can become a terrible mistake for the holder as interest rates rise. *Forget preferred stocks.* If you have any sell them.

New stock issues are coming back as a way of making easy money. In the late sixties, a lot of money was made by the purchase and immediate sale of new stocks that came out and went to an immediate premium. The new issue market collapsed in 1969 largely because so many companies went public with few real assets and with grossly overpriced stocks, but in 1978 there was a definite rebirth in the new issue market. It is likely new issues will have another boom as the inflation speeds up. An example of a new stock issue is illustrated on this page.

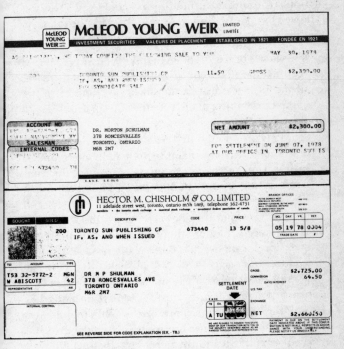

There are two advantages to hot new issues. One is the chance to make a profit without any risk and the second is the fact that your capital is not tied up for more than one or two days. Also there is no commission paid on the purchase. These issues are much sought after and are hard to get so brokers usually dole them out to their good customers. If your broker hasn't cut you in on such goodies, you should try another broker.

One final warning about stock investment. You are running the risk of being taken by traders who take illegal advantage of insider information. In 1978, Robert Bleiberg wrote in *Barron's* that, "illegal trading on inside information is running riot up and down Wall Street". This was followed by an article on August 19, 1978 by Nicholas von Hoffman in *The Washington Post* in which he said:

> This law is broken so often that the Wall Street Journal reported there is circumstantial evidence that there was illegal insider traffic in the stocks of 27 out of 30 U.S. companies subject to merger offers in April and May of this year alone.
>
> Many also don't buy because Wall Street has gone out of its way to merchandise itself as an international casino. Along with the executives of many of the companies whose stock Wall St. sells, brokers have pushed the idea of buying as a gamble on future price rises so long and so loud they have convinced the world that owing stock is a leisure-time activity, an entertainment diversion for money you don't really need and can afford to lose.
>
> Stockholders see their money sunk into bombastically designed, horrendously expensive headquarters buildings and into fancy private jets. They look at their shrunken, misshapened investments, their flat dividend cheques and listen to the screaming about ending tax deductions on the three-martini lunch. They know the government only picks up half the tab for those drinks and they also know who picks up the rest, so they sell out and buy bonds or real estate or antique toys — anything that will hold its value.

To which I can only add — Amen.

Stock Advisory Services

There is an amazing amount of information, misinformation, advice, and misadvice churned out from Wall Street and Bay Street. Much of it is in the form of analysis of different stocks put out by the research departments of the larger brokerage houses, and most of this is reasonably accurate if not of particular value. The problem with these is that by the time the customer actually receives the information sheet it has already gone through far too many hands. Even if the information was of real value, too many people have already acted upon it.

As for advisory services, forget them. The people running them are often unqualified and/or unprincipled and an amazing number of "puff" stocks have been pushed up and out using this route. There are some honest and good services, but the average investor finds it impossible to tell the good from the bad. I write for one service which I think is pretty good, but it is basically a course on investing, not a tip sheet.

In 1977, I had the great pleasure of interviewing one Dr. H. S., a famous stock advisor who says he charges his investors $2,500 per year for his advice which he assured my audience was worth many times that figure. I then confronted Dr. S. with his market letter from exactly one year earlier in which his commodity recommendations had all gone the wrong way; the ones he said to buy had gone down and the ones he suggested selling had gone up! Needless to say Dr. S. was not pleased with me.

And Dr. S. is no worse in his recommendations than dozens of others. What it boils down to is that this is a sucker's game. Save your money and don't subscribe.

Gambling with Ginnie Maes

GNMAs (Government National Mortgage Association Certificates or Ginnie Maes as they are more affectionately called) are 12 year U.S. mortgages which in today's financial climate offer an opportunity to make a great deal of money. Normally mortgages are sold on an individual property, but GNMAs represent a pool of tens of thousands of mortgages divided into $100,000 pieces.

Each GNMA theoretically yields 8% per annum, but in practice the true yield will vary with prevailing interest rates. As mortgage interest rates go up, the value of GNMAs goes down. If interest rates rise over 8%, the price at which each GNMA can be sold will fall below $100,000 until the $8,000 interest paid each year comes in line with current mortgage rates. Suppose mortgages are currently 8% and a GNMA is sold for $100,000. Six months later suppose that interest rates have risen and the GNMA holder wishes to sell. The GNMA will sell at a figure yielding 9%, i.e. the face value is still $100,000 but it will bring on the market only about $90,000. ($8,000 interest on a $90,000 investment is approximately 9%.)

Unlike ordinary mortgages, GNMAs trade on an exchange and their current price is listed every day in the financial newspapers. Here is a sample listing:

GNMA 8% (CBT)—$100,000 prncpl; pts., 32nds of 100%							
	Open	High	Low	Settle	Chg	Close	Yield Chg	Open Interest
Dec	....	....	....	....	....	....	....	336
Mar	87-31	88-01	87-26	87-27	+ 3	9.758	— .015	6,486
June	88-01	88-04	87-29	87-30	+ 3	9.743	— .015	7,124
Sept	88-09	88-13	88-05	88-05	+ 2	9.708	— .010	6,012
Dec	88-14	88-15	88-09	88-10	+ 3	9.682	— :016	6,809
Mar80	88-13	88-13	88-05	88-05	+ 3	9.708	— .015	7,058
June	88-07	88-07	88-01	88-01	+ 1	9.728	— .005	8,638
Sept	88-05	88-05	87-30	87-30	+ 1	9.743	— .005	8,492
Dec	88-01	88-02	87-27	87-27	....	9.758	....	6,192
Mar81	87-30	87-30	87-21	87-21	— 2	9.789	+ .011	3,688
June	87-26	87-26	87-19	87-19	....	9.799	....	1,680
Sept	....	....	....	87-16	....	9.814	....	73
Est vol 4,542; vol Thu 5,245; open int 62,588, +446.							

GNMA Certificates Listing from The Globe and Mail.

Note that the price is quoted in terms of $1 not $100,000. This is just for brevity. GNMAs fluctuate by thirty-seconds of a point and each $1/32$ represents $1/32$ of $1,000, or about $31. A move from 100 to 101 is really a move from $100,000 to $101,000 and represents a difference of $1,000. Note that the September 1979 GNMAs closed at $88 $5/32$ up $2/32$ on the day, i.e. each owner saw his investment rise in value by $62 that day. Note also that GNMAs trade by months. The month named is the month that the mortgage actually begins. You will see that in the further away months, the price is lower. This is because it is widely expected that interest rates will rise in the future; thus GNMAs will fall in price.

How can one make money on mortgages? Certainly not by buying them. As I pointed out earlier, mortgages are a terrible investment in inflationary times. Profits lie in *selling* mortgages. But how does one sell something one does not own? It works something like selling a stock short.

Look again at the sample quotation listing. The June GNMAs closed that day at 87.30 which means someone bought a June GNMA for $87,900 and someone sold at the same price. But a June GNMA is a mortgage beginning the following June. Not until June does delivery take place nor does the mortgage begin to bear interest. What the two people have traded is the intention to carry out a transaction next June and because the mortgage is not yet in existence, the money need not be put up until June — ten months later. Instead each party deposits the sum of $2,000 with their broker as a guarantee. Anytime before next June, the buyer may sell his GNMA or the seller may buy back a similar GNMA, unloading the transaction except for whatever profit or loss may have ensued.

Because only $2,000 is being put down on a $87,000 transaction (a little over 2%) the leverage is very high. If that GNMA moves to 89 from 87, the buyer's $2,000 will have doubled to $4,000, while the seller will have lost his entire stake. Similarly, if the GNMA drops to 85 from 87 the buyer will have lost his $2,000 , while the seller will have doubled his money.

Because of the high leverage, this is not investing and it is not speculating. It is *gambling*. The sale of GNMAs is a gamble with a lot going for it because inflation inevitably results in high interest rates and higher interest rates will inevitably produce much lower prices for GNMAs.

The risk lies in the short term fluctuation. It will do you no good to see GNMAs at a low of 80 one year from now if you are wiped out next week in a quick three day move upwards. One can bet that there will always be short term upward moves when the government finds it advisable politically to artificially force down the interest rates in an attempt to cure a bulge in unemployment or just prior to an election.

If you can afford a gamble and can sit out short-term fluctuations, I strongly recommend the sale of GNMAs at anywhere near their current levels. But if prices are way down before you read this book, then it is too late. After you have sold, put in an order to buy in if they move up two points — in other words limit your loss to $2,000. If they start to move down stay with it and pyramid. If you lose the first time round, try again when the price stabilizes. The idea is to limit your losses and let your profits rise.

Pyramiding is illustrated below:

The first sales of GNMA were made at an average of 90 $^6/_{32}$. When the price reached 89 $^{31}/_{32}$ the paper profit was used to sell another GNMA. This increases the leverage many times and allows the opportunity to make huge sums from a small stake. If the June GNMAs were to move from 87 down to 76, this would increase the original $2,000 stake to $108,000 if completely pyramided.

I cannot stress strongly enough that GNMAs are gambling and very complex. *GNMAs are not for the novice*. But if you are going to gamble, I can think of few better chances for massive profits from limited capital.

TRADE DATE	BOUGHT	SOLD	COMMODITY		SETTLEMENT PRICE	DEBIT	CREDIT
			BEGINNING LEDGER BALANCE				2,173.91
78-08-11		2	79JUN GINNIE MAE	906.875			---*****
78-08-14		1	79JUN GINNIE MAE	905.312			
78-08-14		1	79JUN GINNIE MAE	907.187			
78-08-15		1	79JUN GINNIE MAE	904.062			
78-08-16		1	79JUN GINNIE MAE	899.375			

Whatever Happened to Convertible Bonds?

Nothing illustrates recent changes in the investment climate better than convertible bonds. In 1966, I was describing convertible bonds as "the ideal investment" combining safety of capital together with a steady return and the possibility of capital gains. Today they are almost irrelevant to both investor and speculator. It is not that convertible bonds have changed, for they still have all the same characteristics that made them such a good vehicle in the sixties. No, it is the world around them that has changed — inflation has taken them right out of the picture.

A convertible bond is similar to any other corporation bond in that it is issued by a company in order to raise funds. It is a direct obligation of that company, it pays regular interest on the loan, and it must be repaid by a certain date, usually ten years later. Where the convertible varies from other bonds is that for a stated period during the life of that bond, the holder has the option to turn it in for common stock of the company at a price set at the time of issue and which is usually about 10% higher than the then market price. For example, Whisky Oil Co. stock is trading at $18.50 per share and the company issues 10 million dollars worth of 8% ten year bonds with each $1,000 bond being convertible into fifty shares of common stock at any time during the life·of the bond. Obviously there would be no point in immediate conversion because the stock would end up costing $20 per share and it can be bought on the open market at $18.50. So the buyer holds his bond and draws the 8% interest. But suppose one year later Whisky Oil makes a great strike and the stock moves up to $25 per share. Now the conversion feature becomes of great value and since each bond can be changed into 50 shares, the $1,000 bond is now worth 50 times $25 or $1,250. In other words, if the stock goes down or stays the same the holder just acts as though he has an ordinary bond, but if the stock goes up he reaps in large capital gains.

The reason convertibles are no longer an ideal investment is the same one that has ruined the attractiveness of ordinary bonds. Where the convertible holder originally had two fairly attractive options — make capital gains or sit still and draw interest — he now finds that one of the options is a disaster. Sitting still and drawing interest in inflationary times quickly destroys the investment. In other words, convertible bonds *per se* are no longer a good investment, but individual convertibles may still be attractive depending on the merits of the underwriting corporation. In other words, if a solid oil company, gold mine, or uranium company were to issue a convertible it might be more attractive to buy the convertible rather than the common stock.

This is because convertibles have two major advantages over common stock. Firstly, the commissions are much smaller than on a comparable amount of stock. For example, if you buy $5,000 worth of convertibles, the commission will vary between $12.50 and $37.50 depending on the broker, but the commission on the same amount of stock will be somewhere between $70 and $100. Besides actually saving money, convertibles allow a speculator to trade profitably on very small moves.

Secondly, the amount of money required is much smaller than with stocks because only 25% margin (or less) is required instead of the 50% with stocks. This can result in very large and rapid profits. Here is an example.

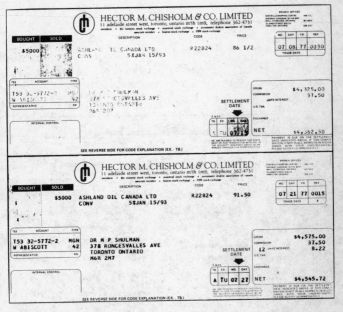

I was very pleased with my $190 profit on a $1,000 investment in just 13 days, but looking back I now realize I wasn't quite as smart as I had thought. One year later, those same bonds that I had proudly sold at $91.50 went all the way up to $200! Oh well, no use crying over a profit.

Oil convertibles have been almost a sure source of profit. If you get a chance to get in on a new issue of oil convertibles grab it, for it's amazing how rapidly profits can ensue. Here is one where I did fairly well.

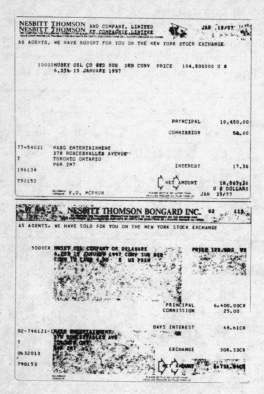

There is another type of convertible bond that is still issued and that makes sense because it gives the buyer an edge and this is the type of bond that is convertible into another currency. Here are three examples of U.S. bonds which are convertible into German marks. Note that the interest rates are low but this is far overshadowed by the potential profit in foreign currency.*

3½%	Olympus Optical (11/1/85)	(DM)	93.75
3½%	Asahi Optical (4/1/87)	(DM)	84.25
3½%	Konishiroku (4/21/85)	(DM)	81.75

In summary, although convertibles are no longer the ideal investment, they still represent the chance to make a good profit *on certain occasions*. Buy them only if the underlying stock is one that you would buy if there was no convertible, but never, never, buy one just because it is a convertible bond.

* The market in these bonds is called by Drexel Burnham Lambert, 60 Broad Street, New York.

Options: Strictly for Fools

Listed options are just that: options to buy or sell stock which is listed on a stock exchange. A list of all the options trading appears every day in *The Wall Street Journal* and other financial papers.

Listed options are the successors to puts and calls, but there are more listed options being traded every day than the old puts and calls brokers used to sell in a week. On the Chicago Board alone, an incredible 100,000 options trade daily and there are over 2 million outstanding. Equally astonishing figures are coming from the other exchanges.

There are three reasons for the great popularity of options. Firstly, they are the newest game in town and have received a great deal of favourable publicity with frequent stories of 50¢ options going to $15 in one week. Secondly, they are extremely popular with one particular group of people — the brokers who handle the buying and the selling — because they are making a small fortune out of them. And finally, they are being traded in such volume mostly because the public is stupid and has bought a phony bill of goods.

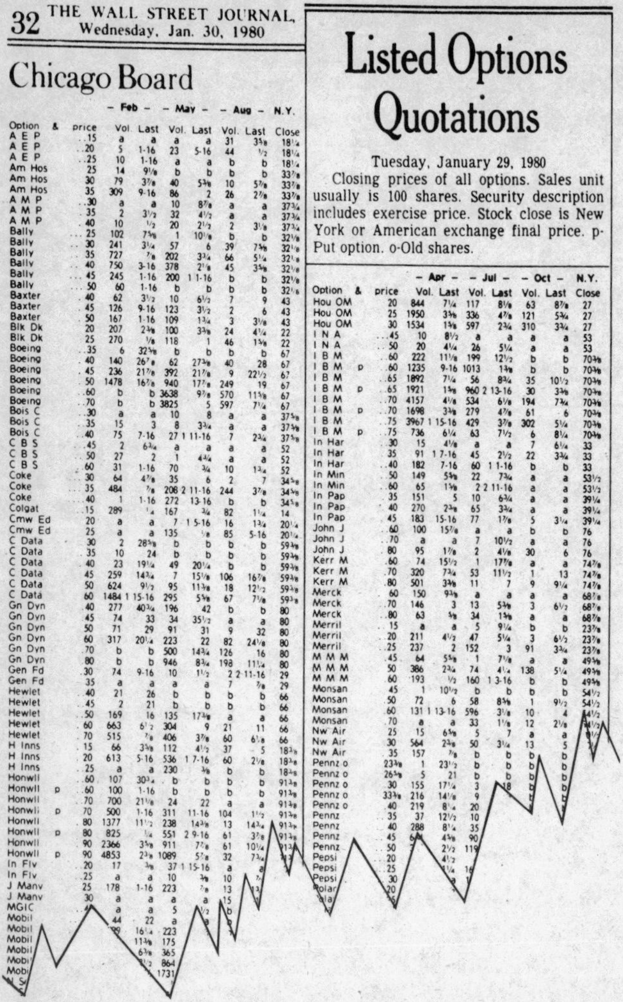

Chicago Board

Option & price	Feb Vol	Last	May Vol	Last	Aug Vol	Last	N.Y. Close
A E P	.15	a	a	a	a	31	3⅛	18¼
A E P	.20	5	1-16	23	5-16	44	½	18¼
A E P	.20	10	1-16	a	a	b	b	18¼
Am Hos	25	14	9⅛	b	b	b	b	33⅞
Am Hos	30	79	3⅝	40	4⅝	10	5⅜	33⅞
Am Hos	35	309	9-16	86	2	26	2⅞	33⅞
A M P	.30	a	10	8⅞	a	a		32½
A M P	.35	2	3½	32	4½	a	a	32½
A M P	.40	10	1-20	20	2½	2	3¼	32½
Bally	.25	102	7⅜	1	10⅛	b	b	32¼
Bally	.30	241	3¼	57	6	39	7¾	32¼
Bally	.35	727	⅞	202	3¾	66	5¼	32¼
Bally	.40	750	3-16	378	2⅛	45	3¾	32¼
Bally	.45	245	1-16	200	1 1-16	b	b	32¼
Bally	.50	60	1-16	b	b	b	b	32¼
Baxter	.40	62	3½	10	6½	7		43
Baxter	.45	126	9-16	123	3½	2	4	43
Baxter	.50	167	1-16	109	1¾	3	3⅛	43
Blk Dk	.20	207	2¾	100	3¾	24	4¼	22
Blk Dk	.25	270	⅛	118	1	46	1¾	22
Boeing	.35	6	32⅜	b	b	b	b	67
Boeing	.40	140	26⅞	62	27⅜	40	28	67
Boeing	.45	236	21⅞	392	21⅞	9	22½	67
Boeing	.50	1478	16⅝	940	17⅜	249	19	67
Boeing	.60	b	b	3638	9⅞	570	11⅜	67
Boeing	.70	b	b	3825	5	597	7¼	67
Bois C	.30	a	10	8	a	a		37⅜
Bois C	.35	15	3	8	3¼	a	a	37⅜
Bois C	.40	75	7-16	2	1 11-16	7	2¾	37⅜
C B S	.45	2	6¾	a	a	a		52
C B S	.50	27	2	1	4¼	a	a	52
C B S	.60	31	1-16	70	¾	10	1¾	52
Coke	.30	64	4⅝	35	¾	2	a	34⅝
Coke	.35	484	⅛	208	2 11-16	244	3⅞	34⅝
Coke	.40	1	1-16	272	13-16	b	b	34⅝
Colgat	.15	289	¼	167	¾	82	1¼	14
Cmw Ed	.20	a	7	1 5-16	16	1¾		20¼
Cmw Ed	.25	a	a	135	⅛	85	5-16	20¼
C Data	.30	2	28½	b	b	b	b	59⅜
C Data	.35	10	24	b	b	b	b	59⅜
C Data	.40	23	19¼	49	20¼	b	b	59⅜
C Data	.45	259	14¼	7	15⅛	106	16⅝	59⅜
C Data	.50	624	9⅝	95	11⅜	18	12½	59⅜
C Data	.60	1484	1 15-16	295	5⅝	67	7⅛	59⅜
Gn Dyn	.40	277	40¼	196	42	a	a	80
Gn Dyn	.45	74	33	34	35½	a	a	80
Gn Dyn	.50	71	29	91	31	9	32	80
Gn Dyn	.60	317	20¼	223	22	82	24¼	80
Gn Dyn	.70	b	b	500	14¾	126	16	80
Gn Dyn	.80	b	b	946	8¼	198	11¼	80
Gen Fd	.25	74	9-16	10	1½	2	2 11-16	29
Gen Fd	.30	74	9-16	a	a	a	a	29
Hewlet	.40	21	26	b	b	b	b	66
Hewlet	.45	2	21	b	b	b	b	66
Hewlet	.50	169	16	135	17¾	a	a	66
Hewlet	.60	663	6½	304	9	21	11	66
Hewlet	.70	515	⅛	406	3⅞	60	6¼	66
H Inns	.15	66	3⅜	112	4½	37	5	18¼
H Inns	.20	613	5-16	536	1 7-16	60	2⅞	18¼
H Inns	.25	a	230	⅜	b	b		18¼
Honwll	.60	107	30¾	b	b	b	b	91⅜
Honwll p	.60	100	1-16	b	b	b	b	91⅜
Honwll	.70	700	21⅛	24	22	a	a	91⅜
Honwll p	.70	500	1-16	311	11-16	104	11½	91⅜
Honwll	.80	1377	11½	238	14¾	13	14¼	91⅜
Honwll p	.80	825	⅛	551	2 9-16	61	3⅞	91⅜
Honwll	.90	2366	3⅞	911	7¾	81	10¾	91⅜
Honwll p	.90	4853	2¾	1089	5½	32	7¾	91⅜
In Flv	.20	17	⅜	37	1 15-16	a	a	22
In Flv	.25	a	10	¼	10	½		22
J Manv	.20	178	1-16	223	⅞	13	½	33¼
J Manv	.30	a	a	a	a			33¼
MGIC	.20	a	5	5	13¾			22⅜
Mobil	.40	44	22	a				23
Mobil	.45		16¼	223	b			
Mobil	.50		11¾	175				
Mobil	.60		6¾	365				
Mobil				864				
Mobil				1731				

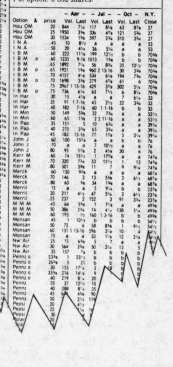

Listed Options Quotations

Tuesday, January 29, 1980

Closing prices of all options. Sales unit usually is 100 shares. Security description includes exercise price. Stock close is New York or American exchange final price. p-Put option. o-Old shares.

Option & price	Apr Vol	Last	Jul Vol	Last	Oct Vol	Last	N.Y. Close
Hou OM	20	844	7¼	117	8⅛	63	8⅞	27
Hou OM	25	1950	3⅝	336	4⅞	121	5¼	27
Hou OM	30	1534	1⅜	597	2¾	310	3¼	27
I N A	.45	10	8½	a	a	a	a	53
I N A	.50	20	4¼	26	5¼	a	a	53
I B M	.60	222	11¾	199	12½	b	b	70⅜
I B M p	.60	1235	9-16	1013	1⅜	a	a	70⅜
I B M	.65	1892	7¼	56	8¾	35	10½	70⅜
I B M p	.65	1921	1⅝	960	2 13-16	30	3⅜	70⅜
I B M	.70	4157	4⅛	534	6½	194	7¾	70⅜
I B M p	.70	1698	3⅝	279	4⅞	61	6	70⅜
I B M	.75	3967	1 15-16	429	3¾	302	5¼	70⅜
I B M p	.75	736	6¼	63	7½	6	8¼	70⅜
In Har	.30	15	4½	a	a	a	a	33
In Har	.35	91	1 7-16	45	2½	22	3¾	33
In Har	.40	182	7-16	60	1 1-16	b	b	33
In Min	.50	149	5⅛	22	7¾	a	a	53½
In Min	.60	65	1⅜	2	2 11-16	a	a	53½
In Pap	.35	151	1	10	6¾	a	a	39¼
In Pap	.40	270	2¾	65	3¾	a	a	39¼
In Pap	.45	183	15-16	77	5	3	3¼	39¼
John J	.60	100	15¾	a	a	b	b	76
John J	.70	a	7	10½	a	a		76
Kerr M	.80	95	1⅞	2	4¾	90	b	74⅞
Kerr M	.60	74	15½	1	17¾	a	a	74⅞
Kerr M	.70	320	7¾	53	11½	1	13	74⅞
Kerr M	.80	501	3⅜	11	7	9	9¼	74⅞
Merck	.60	150	9⅞	a	a	a	a	68⅞
Merck	.70	146	3	13	5⅜	3	6⅞	68⅞
Merck	.80	63	⅝	34	1¾	a	a	68⅞
Merril	.15	a	5	9¼	b	b		23⅞
Merril	.20	211	4½	47	5¾	3	6½	23⅞
Merril	.25	237	2	152	3	91	3¾	23⅞
M M M	.45	64	5¼	1	7¾	a	a	49¼
M M M	.50	386	2¾	74	4¼	138	5¼	49¼
M M M	.60	193	½	160	1 3-16	b	b	49¼
Monsan	.45	1				b	b	49⅞
Monsan	.50	72	5	8¾	1	9½		54½
Monsan	.60	131	1 13-16	5⅞	3¾	10	4	54½
Monsan	.70	70	a	a	3½	1	2½	54½
Nw Air	.25	15	6¾	5	7	a	a	31⅞
Nw Air	.30	564	2¾	50	3½	12	5	31⅞
Nw Air	.35	157	¾	b	b	b	b	31⅞
Pennz o	23⅞	1	23½	b	b	b	b	23⅞
Pennz o	26¾	5	21	b	b			23⅞
Pennz o	33¾	216	14⅞	9				23⅞
Pennz	.30	4	21⅞	8	a			23⅞
Pennz	.35	37	12½	10				23⅞
Pennz	.40	288	8¼	35				23⅞
Pennz	.45	65	4¾	90				23⅞
Pepsi	.20	25	2½	119				
Pepsi	.25		4½	a				
Polar								

Look at the IBM option on the list. It is an option to buy IBM at $60 and it is good until April. The stock closed that day at $70⅜, and 222 options traded with a final closing price of $11⅛. This option is one that is "in the money" because the stock price is higher than the price at which the option can be exercised. Usually option buyers seek out options that are not "in the money", because they are much cheaper and have far higher leverage. Look down the list six more lines and you will see options on the same company at $75, with the one expiring in April trading at only $1 15/16. Now just suppose you bought that option and IBM moved up to $85. Your $1.90 gamble is now worth $10. (Actually they trade in hundreds and your $190 now becomes $1,000.) Wonderful isn't it?

Who sells the options? A few are sold by gamblers who do not own any IBM and are willing to bet that the stock will not move above $75 in the weeks the option has left to run. Most are sold by persons or institutions holding large stock portfolios who are trying to increase their income. It sounds as though the seller can't lose. Suppose you own 100 shares of IBM selling at $70⅜ and you receive $190 for a seventy-day option on your stock. If the stock goes down, stays the same or moves up to $75, the option is not exercised and in seventy days you are back where you were before, still holding your stock but with an extra $190 in your pocket. On the other hand, if the stock moves above $75, the option will be exercised but you will receive $7,500 for your stock plus the $190 you received in advance, giving a net profit of $690 for seventy days. Sound good? Well, don't be in too much of a hurry to phone your broker.

A firm with which I worked did a study of some 150 option buyers and 38 option sellers. Among *all* option buyers, we found that they lost three out of every four times, and those persons buying options *regularly* always ended up as losers. But the most surprising results were concerning the option sellers. Each and every one of them showed a loss after two years of trading!

This really shouldn't be surprising if you stop to think about it. No new money is being created by an option. If the option buyer is betting that the price of the option will rise, then the option seller is betting the opposite. They can't both win. If the stock price drops, the buyer loses his entire stake and if the stock soars and the option buyer makes a huge profit, this is money that the stockholder would have made if he had not sold his option. It is sum game zero. When it is all over the profits of one group must exactly balance the losses of the other. But, in actual fact, they don't and this is the catch 22 of options. In every transaction the broker is taking his commission out of both sides and that money has to come out of someone's pocket.

It is quite different from buying a stock, where if the company does well the price of the stock rises, dividends are paid, and everyone makes money. In options, no new money can be created. If you win, someone else must lose. It's just like a continuous poker game where the house takes 5% out of every pot. After a few hours some will have lost more than others, a few may be temporarily ahead but if they continue to play in that situation sooner or later the house ends up with all the money.

It's fairly obvious why option buyers do badly. Statistically, there is less than a 50% chance that IBM will reach $77.30, which is the break-even point for the option buyer ($75 plus $1.90 plus commissions), so that his occasional profits in a bull market just don't make up for the losses. The problem is that even if he guesses right and IBM moves up 8% in the seventy days all he does is break even. If it just moves up 5%, he loses everything.

Note that it makes no difference if the option buyer

picks a longer running option. The IBM $75 option due next October trades at $5.25 and so the stock must move up much further in order to show a profit. If it goes in the wrong direction, the loss is much higher than with the cheaper option.

The reason option sellers end up as losers is not so clear, but basically they lose because markets are unpredictable. They don't just move up or down, but they gyrate in different directions, often with very short intervals. The result is that holders of stock portfolios who sell options get the worst of both worlds. In falling markets as their stocks go down, they take massive losses cushioned only slightly by the option premium, but in rising markets when they should be making huge profits, the options are exercised and they end up only making 5 or 10% profit on their investment. They limit their profits, but have unlimited losses. The option seller who attempts to trade his stock against the option can be murdered by a whipsawing market. In my more innocent days, I sold an option against Molybdenum and when the stock began to fall sold out my position. Two weeks later, the stock jumped back up above the option price and I was forced to buy it back to protect myself. Finally one week before exercise date, the stock plunged below the option price! The final bill was $26,000.

It's a mugs game! And don't listen to any broker who tells you different. He's making too much out of you to give you honest and disinterested advice.

There is one exception to my advice. If you have inside information on some company and don't mind breaking the law, you can make a great deal of money by buying an option before the public learns the news. It's done every week. A perfect example were the Husky Oil warrants which surged from 50¢ to $13 in July 1978 when Petrocan made a take-over offer. Someone knew ahead of time and bought tens of thousands of warrants in advance of the offer and I presume is now basking in the tropical sun. Despite the frequency of this thievery, securities commissions are curiously reluctant to prosecute and I can't recall a single conviction since the Texas Gulf rip-off in 1968. But if you are an insider and a crook you don't need my advice.

Wine as an Investment

Many people have been forced to eat their words, but this is one area where the great danger is in drinking your investment. It is quite impossible to separate the pleasure of wine from its investment aspect and perhaps this quality adds a special glow to the investment. After all the lucky owner of a case of 1964 Petrus can joyfully drink one of his bottles and reflect that the 11 bottles that are left will still fetch at auction today double what he paid for the case last year. And if all other investments turn sour, wine will remain to give pleasure regardless of the owner's age or infirmity. If only other earthly pleasures persisted as long.

Of course there is wine and there is wine, and most wines are not for investment. Also, wine investment is not for everyone, but if you have already protected yourself against inflation and would now like to be able to ensure pleasure and profit for your declining years, this is how to do it. I don't wish to hurt the sensibilities of American or Canadian patriots who swear by the magnificent qualities of a California Sauterne or a New York red or a British

Columbia white, but regardless of their qualities (and some California wines are magnificent), they are not for investment. You can't make a buck on them, simply because they rarely go up in price. The same applies to Italian wines, Chilean wines, Portugese wines, almost all German wines, and oddly enough most French wines.

What is left? About forty wines from the Bordeaux region, one or two from Burgundy, and perhaps, the rarest wine of all, Trockenbeerenauslese from Germany. We can dispose of the Trockenbeerenauslese quickly enough because its initial high cost ($80 per bottle in a good vintage year) makes upward price movements difficult. If a 1976 Trockenbeerenauslese sells for $80 today, and we expect to at least double our money on our investment every five years, we must look forward to someone being willing to pay $160 in 1984 for a bottle of an eight year-old wine. Maybe it will happen, but I have my doubts.

The same applies to the great Burgundy, Romanée-Conti. This magnificent wine is produced in such small quantities that it is actually rationed to the wine stores. In order to get one case of Romanée-Conti a wine merchant must purchase thirty cases of less remarkable wine. This results in very high prices to the customer ranging from about $70 per bottle in the 1972 vintage to $150 for the 1971 vintage. It's pretty hard to move much higher to allow a profit when prices are so high to start. (A year ago I saw a bottle of 1971 Romanée-Conti offered for sale in a Toronto restaurant for $650. There were no takers.) Anyone who buys Romanée-Conti or Trockenbeerenauslese should not delude himself into calling it an investment — unless it be an investment in pleasure.

And this brings me to profiting in wine. To begin with, one must buy wine that will not go bad as it gets older, that will go up in price, and that can be resold at a profit. Many wines are pasteurized and will live forever but because they are pasteurized they are in effect dead. They are second rate and not worth a second glance — or taste. The non-pasteurized wines will continue to develop and grow in the bottle but will finally die of old age and turn to vinegar. The bottle life of most non-pasteurized wines is surprisingly short. Most whites last a few years at best and Beaujolais and most red Bordeaux don't live much longer. The finest Bordeaux however can last 100 years or even longer and the best of these develop so slowly that they are not even ready to drink for fifteen years and do not reach their peak for twenty-five years. The 1945 wines are an excellent example of these slow developers. They are finally at their peak today and will live for another fifty years (if given the chance).

Bordeaux wines from the Médoc were classified as to quality back in 1855 and the same classification is used today to grade these wines (with one change: Mouton Rothschild was promoted a few years ago from second class to first). There are five classifications and here are all the wines listed:

First Growth

Lafite-Rothschild   Mouton-Rothschild

Margaux   Haut-Brion

Latour

Second Growth

Rauzan-Segla   Lascombes

Rauzan-Gassies   Brane-Cantenac

Léoville-Las-Cases   Pichon-Longueville

Léoville-Poyferré   Pichon-Lalande

Léoville-Barton   Ducru-Beaucaillou

Durfort-Vivens   Cos-d'Estournel

Gruaud-Larose   Montrose

Third Growth

Kirwan, Cantenac
d'Issan, Cantenac
Lagrange, St.-Julien
Langoa-Barton, St.-Julien
Giscours, Labarde
Malescot-St.-Exupéry, Margaux
Cantenac-Brown, Cantenac

Boyd-Cantenac, Margaux
Palmer, Cantenac
La Lagune, Ludon
Desmirail, Margaux
Calon-Segur, St. Estephe
Ferriere, Margaux
Marquis d'Alesme-Becker, Margaux

Fourth Growth

St. Pierre, St.-Julien
Talbot, St.-Julien
Branaire-Ducru, St.-Julien
Duhart-Milon-Rothschild, Pauillac
Pouget, Cantenac

La Tour Carnet, St.-Laurent
Lafon-Rochet, St.-Estèphe
Beychevelle, St.-Julien
Prieuré-Lichine, Canenac
Marquis de Terme, Margaux

Fifth Growth

Pontet-Canet
Batailley
Haut-Batailley
Grand-Puy-Lacoste
Grand-Puy-Ducasse
Lynch-Bages
Lynch-Moussas
Dauzac
Mouton Baron Phillipe

du Tertre
Haut-Bages-Libéral
Pédesclaux
Belgrave
de Camensac
Cos-Labory
Clerc Milon
Croizet-Bages
Cantemerle

There are many excellent wines in the second, third, fourth, and fifth growths. (My favourites are Palmer and Talbot.) But from an investment point of view, it is best to stick to the first growth because there is always a ready market to sell these wines and they tend to increase faster in price than do their lesser neighbours. To these five great wines one should add two equally magnificent wines from the St. Emilion area, Cheval Blanc and Petrus which have been and will continue to be excellent investments and also one sweet wine Chateau Yquem.

Collecting wine is not as easy as collecting Krugerrand. Although wine can be purchased and will be stored at nominal charge by the auction houses, one of the pleasures of wine ownership is keeping it in your own home and for that a cool dark cellar is required where there is reasonable security and minimum temperature fluctuation. Also remember that wine cannot be purchased on the basis of name alone, for the best vineyard will not produce great wine if the weather is bad and Bordeaux weather is always unpredictable. Thus you could have purchased a bottle of 1968 Lafite (a terrible year all over southern France) seven years ago for $5 a bottle and today you would get little more than your $5 back. (But if you had purchased a second growth wine from a bad year it could not be resold at any price.)

Here is a list of vintages as a general guide:

1961	Magnificent. Good for another 100 years.
1962	Average wines. Short life. Not good for investment.
1963	Awful.
1964	Good wines. Buy them if available cheap. Good for another twenty years.
1965	Awful.
1966	Good wines. Good investment. Good for our lifetime.
1967	Fair wines. Short life. Not for investment.
1968	Awful.
1969	Short life. Don't buy them.

1970	Magnificent. Up to now second only to tl 1961. If you can buy these at a fair price, do s
1971	Good wines. Too short lived for investmen
1972	Awful.
1973	Poor.
1974	Poor.
1975	The wines of the century. Buy them.
1976	Good wines. Too soon to judge longevity.
1977	Awful.

It is best to buy younger wines before the prices have soared and probably the best buys for the investor today would be the 1975 and the 1970 vintages. The only problem with the 1975 vintages is that it is unlikely that many of my readers will ever drink these wines for it is generally agreed that these great wines will not be ready for drinking before 1995. The middle-aged among us who buy such wines are really estate planning rather than laying down a wine cellar. The 1970 vintages, on the other hand, will be drinkable in two or three years and will continue to improve for another ten or fifteen years.

The place to buy these wines is not Bordeaux since they are cheaper by a third to a half in New York City. Lafite 1970, for example, is sold at the Chateaux for $60 per bottle and is freely available in New York at less than $40. The reason for this odd situation is the precipitous drop of the U.S. dollar plus the imposition of large local French taxes. This is purely a temporary situation and wine prices have already begun to move up in the U.S. as new imports are brought in.

As for buying old wines or selling your own collection, the best place is Christie's or Sotheby auction houses in London or Heublein in the U.S. For $15 per year Christie's or Sotheby will send out a monthly catalogue listing all the wine for auction with estimated prices and after the sale they will tell you what the wine actually fetched. In addition prior to each sale, they send out a newsletter giving valuable information about the wine available for purchase.

I have found Christie's to be a delight to deal with. Their service is excellent and commissions are very low (10 to 15%). They will either ship your wines or arrange storage.

One other excellent way to make money in wine is to buy for future delivery as soon as it is clear that the vintage is a great one. Thus, in August 1977, the Chicago Wine Company wrote their customers soliciting purchase of the 1975 first growths in these words:

> There has been a tremendous amount of interest and excitement about the 1975 Bordeaux vintage. The weather conditions during 1975 were very similar to what occurred in 1961 — rain in the spring, a dry, hot summer, and near perfect weather during the harvesting. The sugar content of the grapes was high enough to insure wines with an excellent balance of alcohol and acidity.
>
> While no one can guarantee that the wines from all of the Chateaux will be as good as the fabulous 1961's, the reports are that a number of the top classified Chateaux could equal or surpass the 1961's and possibly reach the level of the legendary 1929's and 1945's. As you probably already know, the 1961's are big, complex, long-lived wines that still, in many cases, have not reached their peak. Accordingly, the 1975's are wines to buy now for laying down for several years.

In the same mailing they included the next table to show big profits made in the great vintages of the past.

Prices of Six Top Bordeaux Vintages
(Price per Case Converted to 1976 U.S. Dollars)

Vintage	Lafite Rothschild	Latour	Mouton Rothschild	Margaux
1929				
1st Offering to Importers	$18	$18	$18	$18
2nd Offering to Importers	$25	$22	$22	$22
Percentage Increase	38.9%	22.2%	22.2%	22.2%
1970 London Wholesale	$1,600	$850	$2,000	$500
1945				
1st Offering to Importers	$35	Data	$28	$45
2nd Offering to Importers	$50	not	$40	$50
Percentage Increase	42.9%	avail-	42.9%	11.1%
1970 London Wholesale	$850	able	$600	$600
1959				
1st Offering to Importers	$50	$30	$40	$35
2nd Offering to Importers	$75	$45	$50	$45
Percentage Increase	50.0%	50.0%	25.0%	28.6%
1970 London Wholesale	$800	$550	$625	500
Average 1976 U.S. Retail (Approx.)	$1,380	$720	$1,200	$720
1961				
1st Offering to Importers	$80	$50	$60	$45
2nd Offering to Importers	$100	$90	$95	$75
Percentage Increase	25.0%	80.0%	58.3%	66.7%
1970 London Wholesale	$500	$425	$500	$360
Average 1976 U.S. Retail (Approx.)	$1,200	$1,020	$1,200	$1,02
1966				
1st Offering to Importers	$75	$60	$70	$50
2nd Offering to Importers	$100	$110	$120	$85
Percentage Increase	33.3%	83.3%	71.4%	70.0%
Average 1976 U.S. Retail (Approx.)	$350	$300	$350	$300
1970				
1st Offering to Importers	$110	$75	$115	$80
2nd Offering to Importers	$150	$145	$160	$135
Percentage Increase	36.4%	93.3%	39.1%	68.8%
Average 1976 U.S. Retail (Approx.)	$300	$290	$290	$265

NEWS FROM CHRISTIE'S
WINE DEPARTMENT

Finest & Rarest Wines & Collectors' Pieces - Thursday, September 21, 1978

Foreword

Welcome, loyal old regulars and new subscribers, to the first major wine sale of the new season. In terms of range and quality, it is in the big league. A note about the contents below.

The original purpose of these sale memoranda - the first went out with our catalogue of October 11, 1966 - was to explain the difference between buying wine and works of art   auction, to draw attention to the various services, and to give background information. As we invariably have a batch of new subscribers, and memories tend to be short, I propose to continue along the same lines.

Jet setting connoisseurs

This sale has a code reference 'Concorde II' to honour the small, elite and well-off ($4,746 for 7 days) group who are taking part in this year's 'Concorde' trip. Indeed, the theme 'Concorde to Champagne, Claret and Christie's', is reflected in the catalogue with a particularly good range of old classic vintages of champagne and of both the first growths at which the party will have dined: Lafite and Yquem. After the sale and a couple more banquets, they will wing it, supersonically, back to New York to liver salts and rest.

Contents of catalogue

I hope the general index to sections on the page preceding lot 1 will be a helpful lead-in. Further information follows:

Paris cellar, lots 24/41, 105/125, 153/169, 203/227 are all from a cellar in the heart of that city. The wines were laid down by the father of the present owner, a noted connoisseur. Incidentally, from the same cellar, came the first bottle of 1806 Lafite, taken by us to America for sale in 1976.

Unparalleled range of Lafite, lots 228/247 - a third bottle of the '06 (1806 that is), heads the magnificent collection of Lafite, which has come from another outstanding French cellar. The wines were inspected and packed in the original cellars by ourselves. Just to make one thing quite clear, they are not from Lafite, or from any other Rothschild cellar.

NB: overseas buyers can virtually ignore the dagger signs (necessary because the wine has been imported for sale) as the 8% value added tax is refundable on proof of exportation - we can advise and arrange.

The wine company was right. The Petrus 1975 offered then at $20 has already moved up 50% in price as have all the other first growths. It would have been nice to have bought 1975 futures but it's too late for that. However, 1975 wines are still a good buy today.

What it all boils down to is that wine investment is a luxury because time and patience are needed for prices to rise and will power is essential to keep from drinking the investment. But for a small portion of your funds, this brings a charm that can be found nowhere else in life — and occasionally a most unexpected profit. In January 1980 I discovered that the Liquor Control Board in my area, which normally overcharges everybody, had put La Tàche 1971 (a red burgundy) on sale at $80 a bottle while the same wine was selling simultaneously in London at $150 per bottle. I bought three cases and am torn between cupidity and desire for the wine. Such an unusual windfall couldn't happen in any other investment field.

How much profit can one reasonably expect to make by investing in wine? At the worst your investment should keep up with inflation. With a little luck another boom will develop in French wines and today's $20 bottle of wine could easily go to $100. After all a Latour in a good year should be worth as much as a Romanee Conte or a Trockenbeerenauslese. One thing for sure, because of inflation you won't lose money.

Higher wine prices in France are not an isolated event — the same thing is happening to everything all across Europe. In August 1978, I priced a travelling clock in the Cartier shop in Bordeaux at $285 and one week later saw the same clock in Cartiers New York store for $195. Cartier has not gone crazy. This variance in price is due to the extreme fall in the dollar which shows no sign of stopping.

These discrepencies are temporary and they are not

going to be solved by European prices falling. Instead we are already seeing a flood of German and Swiss tourists taking advantage of our low prices and this will end the same way it did in Britain when the pound fell. Prices in the U.S. will rise to meet foreign levels. If there is something you will have to buy soon, don't wait. It will cost you more next spring.

And this brings me to the most pleasant investment of all — beautiful things.

Art and Antiques:
Investments to Love

The sketch on the previous page was made in Peking in 1780. I bought it four years ago, in 1976, for $10. The shawl cost me $400 in Spain five years ago. It was made in the Philippines immediately after the First World War. The golden cup was made in Russia in 1880 for the Romanovs. Last year it was purchased in Toronto for $2,000. The box was made in 1800 for some wealthy Polish aristocrat. It was bought in New York last year for $7,000.

All of these objects represent the opportunity to profit in coin and pleasure at the same time. The value of the sketch increased tenfold in just three years, and the shawl was worth twice what I paid. The owner of the cup was offered $2,800 only three days after his purchase. And the box was resold for $9,000. Even more important, ownership of such beautiful objects brings constant pleasure and excitement.

The important word in the last paragraph is "beaut-iful", for with the great variety of art and antiques available for investment today, the one group that moves up consistently in price are those that are considered beautiful. It is true that ideas of beauty vary drastically from person to person, but some objects are universally accepted as beautiful — well almost universally. Three years ago I brought out a book on investing in art* and I was amazed at how deep were the passions which I stirred. Some people don't like the thought of anyone buying art in order to profit for they feel it's somehow indecent. This attitude was summed up by a scathing condemnation of my book in an artsy magazine called *Saturday Night* in August 1977.

Art collecting, as Shulman practises it, is itself a parody of capitalism. It is capitalism stripped of all social justifications. It does nothing but turn a profit. It provides no jobs, builds no cities, pays few taxes — Shulman rejoices in the fact that governments haven't yet figured out how to tax art. It doesn't lead to the creation of distinguished collections which can later be enjoyed by whole communities — in this kind of art investing, collections are constantly being broken up, the individual pieces being passed on from collector to dealer to collector. It of course supports no acts of creation; it specifically avoids just that kind of thing, on the grounds of high risk, and thereby surrenders the act of patronage, the main justification for art collecting during the last few centuries. It is capitalism-for-capitalism's sake, a queer kind of inversion of the art-for-art-sake's doctrine that Shulman would probably find abhorrent. *Anyone Can Make Big Money Buying Art*, if it happens to be read by somebody a century from now, will be identified quickly as a mean-minded Marxist's parody of the ac-

Anyone Can Make Big Money Buying Art (New York: Macmillan; Toronto: Fitzhenry & Whiteside, 1977)

quisitive instinct, misleadingly and mischievously issued under the name of a famous millionaire socialist of the day.

And far from finding my art objects beautiful, the writer of the column, one Robert Fulford, lumped them all together as "kitsch".

Well, perhaps I am a philistine by art world standards but I don't think that there is some mortal sin in investing in a painting as compared to a gold bar or in an ancient glass cup instead of a stock certificate. The critics don't like it, but an errant capitalist can get just as much pleasure from a beautiful old Syrian cup as a collector of modern art may get from his dabs of incomprehensible (to me) paint. Anyway, enough of the critics. In a bad inflation there just isn't time to worry about them, and it is an undisputed fact that art has been one of the safest places for capital during bad inflations. Everything else may go to pot, but good art keeps its value.

But what art should one buy? Paintings or sculpture, old furniture or stained glass, armour or silver, Chinese art or Russian art, watches or glass, there is enough variety for every taste. And that answers the question: buy what you like, what turns you on. With so much available, there's no point in collecting things you don't enjoy. But if you want to be sure to profit you must follow certain guidelines, just as in any other type of investment.

First of all, old is better. Don't buy *any* modern art for investment. It's not that our contemporaries won't produce items of lasting value just like every society that has preceded us. It's just that we're too close to the vast mass of today's art to tell what will last and what will not. It was the same with every preceding generation. Just look back to paintings done one hundred years ago; 99% of them are totally unsaleable today even though many of them sold for large sums when first produced. Also today's more prominent living artists are heavily promoted by their supporting galleries and the prices are carefully controlled and pushed upwards to levels that appear totally unreasonable in relation to the prices of the great artists of yesteryears.

Hundertwasser is an example of this trend. This very popular young artist now issues signed engravings with perhaps 300 copies which his New York gallery sells at around $2,000. Compare that to Picasso's *Vollard Suite* of which there were 300 copies made forty-five years ago and which are available for a third less than a Hundertwasser. Or go back a long way to Rembrandt's engravings which sell for as little as $1,000. Such inequities can't last indefinitely and so it's extremely unlikely that anyone buying Hundertwasser today will make a profit. This doesn't mean modern art should never purchased, just never for investment purposes. If something turns you on and you will get sufficient pleasure from it that is a different matter entirely. But don't kid yourself into thinking it's an investment.

Eskimo art is the perfect example of how the public is being deluded into buying vast amounts of merchandise under the impression that it is a good investment. Stories have been carried in the press and on the CBC of prints being bought in 1962 for $60 and being resold for $12,000 in 1979, of people standing in line overnight in order to be sure to purchase a new edition of lithographs, of carvings changing hands at auction for $25,000 and more. The sad fact is that Eskimo art is being ground out in vast quantities in order to satisfy the market. Moreover, it is all marked up over 100% by the retailing galleries, some 99% of the Eskimo art has no resale value and the well-publicized huge prices were not real transactions. We have now reached the point where criticism of this type of "investment" is received very angrily because thousands of people are making a living out of it.

If a piece of Eskimo art pleases you by all means buy it for pleasure, but you should know that the chance of your ever getting your money back is miniscule and the possibility of making a profit is zylch.

Among old things, small is far better than large. Tiny objects appreciate in value anywhere from three to ten times as quickly as unwieldy things. So buy a watch instead of a clock, old jewellery instead of old furniture, snuff boxes instead of old chests. The reason is a basic one. Art for investment is collected by a wide variety of wealthy and not so wealthy individuals, many of whom live in politically unstable areas like the Middle East, and if these collectors have to run they want to be able to take their wealth with them. The people of Europe have learned from repeated wars that many persons who could stuff their valuables into a suitcase saved that wealth (and sometimes their own lives as a result) while persons of similar wealth which was invested in land, furniture and "grand" possessions lost everything. The Junkers of East Prussia are the perfect example. Those who put their wealth into baronial possessions were stripped in 1945, while those who had some of their wealth in small art objects were able to escape with them and begin again in the west with financial resources.

It is unlikely anyone will ever have to flee from Chicago or any other U.S. or Canadian city, but that doesn't matter. Since valuable art objects are internationally auctioned, the higher bids coming from overseas push up the prices in North America as well. It isn't just Europeans and Arabs who want smaller valuables. The people of Canada and Mexico have both seen their currency collapse in recent years and from both countries there has been a flight of wealth plus the accumulation of small precious objects. This may well end with currency controls in both countries and a ban on export of assets. But how can any government keep track of a two or three inch privately owned object, no matter how valuable it may be. Precious small objects are becoming the ultimate refuge for nervous wealth all over the world, and as a result their value goes up steadily as the dollar continues its decline.

Old, small and beautiful. What else should we look for? Innate value certainly helps. Objects containing gold or precious stones are more likely to retain their value in bad times and go up in good times than something like a painting whose value is just in its beauty. Chinese export silver made of pure silver and beautifully enamelled, for example was always saleable for its silver value in China and Hong Kong, even during the 1948 debacle when exquisite paintings and porcelain vases were simply abandoned. I purchased the set of silver spoons shown above from the Chinese government for their weight in silver ($70) just four years ago when that country was selling off so much of its art. Today it would bring at least ten times that figure.

Beware of fakes. This is the great pitfall in art investing and is amazingly common. No one need ever get stuck with a fake, for local museums are happy to authenticate (but not evaluate) any object. And of course you should not be buying for investment in any antique store, even the best. Their mark-up is too high to leave room for you to profit and prices must go up by at least 50% before you are back to even. The two big advantages in buying from the big international auctioneers are that prices are basically at the wholesale level. There is also no danger of buying a fake because the auctioneers give a guarantee of authenticity. You have five years to claim your money if it turns out the piece is not real.

The New York addresses of the three big international auction houses that sell to the public are:

Phillips, 867 Madison Ave., New York 10021.

Sotheby Parke Bernet, 980 Madison Ave., New York 10021.

Christie, Manson & Woods, 502 Park Ave., New York 10022.

Each of these companies will be happy to put readers on their mailing list of forthcoming sales at no charge. Individual catalogues may be purchased, or for a few dollars a subscription may be ordered for all the sales in the desired field.

The one reason to justify buying in antique shops is to fill out a particular hole in a collection, or because an object is so beautiful that temporary overpayment is worthwhile. Over the years, I have purchased several such magnificent and unique pieces from the likes of A La Vielle Russe or Skalas in New York, Wartski in London and Au Vieux Cadran in Paris and have ended up with my acquisition being worth far more than I paid, because in inflation the best pieces go up the fastest.

And that is very important. Regardless of the price range you are working in, always buy the best piece available that you can afford. Second rate art works are hard to get rid of and slow to appreciate, but there is always a ready market for the best.

How much return should one expect from an investment in art? Profits can be fantastically large here, higher than in any other field. But patience is necessary and it is rare to turn something over in a few days. For the investor who is prepared to wait for three to five years amazing profits are possible. The largest profit I ever made in the stock market was in a little company called Canada Foils when my $350 investment turned into $16,500. That great gain looks small beside the watch I bought for $250 and sold for $65,000! That was of course highly unusual but an astute art investor should do at least as well as the investor in land or gold. He has one extra advantage that can be found no where else: he can guarantee a profit.

The way to do this is to work closely with your local museum. Buy things that your museum wants to own (every museum curator is happy to advise on buying such objects), retain and enjoy your purchase for two or three years while inflation pushes up their price and then donate them to the museum and take a tax deduction. You will be allowed a valuation dependent on the current fair retail market value of the art object. If you have bought reasonably at auction you can make just as big a profit this way as by resale — and with no risk!

And as inflation speeds up profits in art will increase ever more rapidly. *Barron's* magazine of November 12, 1979 reported:

A new world record auction price for a surrealist painting was set last Monday night at Sotheby Parke Bernet (SPB). Before a standing-room-only audience, a 39-by-98.5-inch work by Man Ray, entitled "A L'Heure de L'Observatoire: Les Amoureux" and painted in 1932-1934, was hammered down for the amazing sum of $750,000. The pre-sale estimate was $200,000-$250,000.

In summary, art investment offers the excellent possibility of huge profits associated with many dividends in the form of pleasure. Of course, there is always the chance of falling in love with your purchase and then selling becomes too painful. The most beautiful thing I own is a lovely eighteenth century pendant made of pearls and filigree gold with a seven day watch on its back. Made originally for a mistress of Louis XVI and sold for the equivalent of $180 dollars (equivalent to many tens of thousands of today's dollars), it disappeared during the revolution and reappeared after World War II. In 1945, it was brought to a

Parisian dealer, Madame Aug Seiler, by a French general's widow and she purchased it for 800 francs (about $200). Ten years later a famous New York watch shop owner named Mr. Barney saw the piece at Madame Seiler's and bought it for $350. In 1964, I bought it from him for $1,000. Two years ago, I turned down a $100,000 offer for the pendant.

Where else can an investor find such romance and excitement?

Oil and Taxes:
For Millionaires Only

It is obvious that if one is to move ahead financially, tax payments should be kept to the minimum legally possibly. I have touched on cutting taxes and making a profit by giving away art objects to the local museum. There are many other legal gimmicks available to reduce income taxes, such as investing in movie productions, and these will be discussed later in the next chapter. There is one method, however, that is intimately tied in with inflation and "wealth in the ground" that will be given consideration here — investing in oil drilling.

Governments recognize the necessity of increasing our oil and gas reserves and for that purpose encourage exploration by giving generous tax write-offs to persons who invest money in this field. As a result, oil drilling has become a very, very attractive speculation today. To make clear how very attractive it is, let us suppose an investor puts $5,000 into shares of the XYZ oil company listed on the

New York exchange and the company goes broke. The end result is simply that the investor has lost his $5,000 and there is no compensation available to him, although he may deduct that $5,000 from any capital gain he has made when computing his capital gain tax. Let us suppose, instead, that that same investor takes his $5,000 and invests it into a private oil drilling fund which also goes broke. The end result here is quite different. Under current laws the entire $5,000 can be deducted from the investor's income before calculating his tax so that the government actually pays over half of the loss!

The actual amount depends on the type of drilling fund in which you invest. There are two types of drilling funds, those that drill in western Canada and the so-called frontier funds that drill in the Arctic or off the East Coast. The western funds allow 100% deduction from your income before calculating tax and they carry an excellent chance of making a profit. The frontier funds will probably never find commercial oil but they allow the investor to deduct up to 166% of his investment. Of course some of these benefits could be affected by future federal budgets.

This chapter is headed "for millionaires only" because private drilling funds don't want to bother with small investors. Most of them will take only minimum investments of $50,000 or $100,000, although there are a few which will take as little as $5,000.

In the fall of 1978, I was approached by the President of the Alberta Stock Exchange, Bob Peters, who urged me to put $100,000 in a new private drilling fund being underwritten by his company. The fund is called Sceptre Resources Partnership. It is run by a general partner in the form of a well established public company called Sceptre Resources, which is active in the oil drilling and development business in western Canada. Its stock is listed on the

Toronto Stock Exchange. The set-up is quite typical of such funds. Twenty-five or more limited partnerships were being sold at $100,000 each. Sceptre Resources uses the money plus their own funds, in the ratio of 70% from the limited partners and 30% from Sceptre Resources, to buy land and drill wells. All revenue is shared equally by Sceptre Resources and the limited partners. If Sceptre loses, the loss is deductible from the investors' income tax.

It is very intriguing, but obviously no one goes into an investment expecting to lose and take a tax deduction, so the key is really what are the chances of profit? It all boils down to with whom you are investing. I examined the record of Bob Peters' seven previous drilling funds and was amazed to discover that so far all of these have been profitable, so that none of his investors has had to depend on the tax deduction. His past funds were as follows:

(1) Kildonan 1976 Fund. Now earning $200,000 per year for every $100,000 invested. $600,000 was originally invested and another $1,900,000 was borrowed. Over the next twelve years, it is forecast that this will grow to $11,000,000.

(2) Kildonan 1977 Fund. The two million dollars put in this fund are still being spent. But already they have successfully drilled one oil well and three gas wells. The success so far indicates that the investors will have all their own money back by 1983.

(3) Concept Drilling Partnership. This fund was started only one year ago, but already they have proven up and capped a gas field worth at least double the original investment.

(4) Westlock Joint Venture. This fund was organized in late 1976 to take advantage of Alberta's income tax in-

centive cash rebates. Individuals in the 58% personal income tax bracket ended up having no after-tax investment in this program. To date, sales from the fund have totalled $625,000. Earned depletion of $200,000 is available from resource income to a maximum of 25% resulting in a taxable income of $475,000. Thus, after tax, investors ended up earning $249,500. Subsequent sales will increase the percentage return from this wonderful investment where the invested capital is zero.

(5) Willesden Green Joint Venture. This program is identical in structure to the Westlock program, but has not been as financially rewarding. The pretax investment of $225,000 again worked out to zero after-tax investment. However, revenues on this smaller program have totalled only $90,000 to date.

(6) CRA Ocelot Fund. The CRA Ocelot Fund has been sold to the operator for a gross 20% pretax return and estimated (depending upon individual income tax rate) 35% after-tax return.

(7) CRA Exploration 78 Program. Although this fund is only a year old, it has already drilled three successful wells. The investors are sure of a profit.

Obviously not every drilling fund is going to have Bob Peters' success — nor is he likely to continue to bat a thousand. I asked Peters what rules he lays down for his funds and he listed six:

(1) The programs must have the potential for a minimum annual 20% after-tax return.

(2) The operator must share the monetary risk associated with the expected return.

(3) The underwriters must invest their pretax dollars

alongside and on the same basis as the investors.

(4) All funding should be done via private placements to avoid the time loss and cost of regulatory scrutiny. (I don't agree with this. Regulation is needed to protect against crooks.)

(5) The sharing of the reward after the investor has recovered his capital cost is weighted in the investor's favour, not that of the operator and/or the promoter.

(6) The operator-manager of the program represents the best talent available.

My rules to success in this exciting investment field are simple:

(1) It helps to be in a high tax bracket.

(2) You must have a large amount of cash available that can be tied up for several years. You can't sell out like a stock.

(3) All these funds have a general partner who manages the pot. The key to whether you invest should be the track record of the general partner.

(4) Look at the prospectus and see if the underwriter has invested his own money. If the deal is a fair one, he should be willing to risk his own funds.

Anyone following these rules in a drilling fund is likely to get very rich. At the worst, the Canadian Government will be happy to share the losses.

Tax Avoidance

No one likes to pay income tax and an amazing number of Canadians evade paying their share through fraud — reporting non-existent children, charging household expenses to the office, or deducting car expenses which had nothing to do with business. Needless to say I do not recommend such practices because the government tends to be very nasty with tax evaders. However, tax avoidance and minimization is another matter entirely and it is only common sense to pay the minimum tax required. While the oil shelters I discussed in the last chapter are of interest only to those in the highest tax brackets, there are others that should be discussed.

MURBs (multiple unit residential buildings) and motion pictures are Canada's most common type of tax shelter and I cannot recommend either — MURBs because inflation and rent control can play havoc with the ownership of apartment buildings (see page 48) and motion pictures because almost inevitably the investor gets ripped off in such vehicles. Three years ago, a friend backed a popular Canadian film which cost less than $250,000 to produce and the movie grossed eight million dollars, yet the investors didn't make a cent because everyone from the distributor to the theatre owner got their hand into the till. The actors did well, the producers made money, the distributor made a fortune and the exhibitor sold out. But when the smoke cleared the investors were considered lucky to get their investment back! And this movie was an unusual success! Stay away from movies — they are a suckers' investment.

As for RRSPs it amazes me how many otherwise sensible people are sinking today's relatively good dollars into pension plans that will pay off in twenty or thirty years. The rationale is that no taxes are paid on contributions until they are withdrawn from the plan in the future and in the meantime the monies pile up interest. In normal times an RRSP would make sense, but in inflationary times most pension plans are no good for the same reason bonds are no good. They will pay off in worthless paper money.

The only pension plans that make any sense are those that are self-managed and in which the money is invested in inflation-proof things, but the government does everything it can to prevent such investments. There are prohibitions against placing gold or real estate in RRSPs and so the only good outlets are "wealth in the ground" stocks like Noranda, Inco, Dome Mines, Campbell Red Lake and Brascan. Let me repeat, *RRSPs only make sense if the monies deposited are used to buy inflation-proof investments.*

There are other ways to minimize income tax. My accountant, Wm. Eisenberg & Co. prepared for their clients a guide to the methods available. With their permission, I have reprinted it here.

Savings through Tax Deferral

Registered home ownership savings plans (RHOSP)

This popular technique allows you to save tax free to purchase a home. If you wish to take advantage of this technique, this is how you qualify:

- You must be resident in Canada and eighteen years of age or over.
- You may only make a deductible contribution to a RHOSP for the [1980] year if neither you nor your spouse owned a home anywhere in the world in [1980 *and* 1979].
- You may contribute up to $1,000 per year to your RHOSP. The maximum deductible contributions that you may make in a lifetime are $10,000.
- Your contribution must be made before January 1, [1981, to be deductible from 1980 income].
- You may only have one RHOSP in a lifetime. Once you have established a RHOSP the plan itself has a maximum lifetime of 20 years.

If you borrowed money to contribute to the RHOSP, the interest on the borrowed funds will not be deductible.

If you terminate your RHOSP in a particular taxation year, the funds received will be taxable in the year unless you use the funds to buy a home in Canada or to buy an income averaging annuity contract (see comments on income averaging annuity contracts below). However, if you purchase a home within three years after the year in which you terminate your RHOSP, you will be able to obtain a deduction in the year you purchase the home to the extent that an amount equal to the RHOSP funds previously included in your income was applied to the purchase price of your home.

If you have a child over 18 who would qualify as a dependent in [1980], but for the fact that the child had net income greater than $2,750 [or the maximum in 1980], you might give consideration to your child contributing to a RHOSP in order to reduce his income.

Income averaging annuity contracts (IAAC)

An IAAC is designed to permit you to spread over a number of years the tax on certain types of income which tend to create a significant increase in your income in the year. The types of income receipts which are eligible for transfer into an IAAC include:

- taxable capital gains
- income from the production of literary, dramatic, musical or artistic work
- income earned as an athlete, musician or public entertainer
- lump-sum payments received from a company pension plan
- retiring allowances and payments in respect of loss of office
- death benefits
- a refund of premiums from an RRSP on the death of the annuitant
- recapture of capital cost allowance
- employee stock option benefits
- amounts received from a RHOSP.

If you have qualifying income you must include the full amount in your income for the year. Then, if you buy an IAAC, you may deduct the cost of that investment (up to the amount of the qualifying income less one year's annuity payments on the IAAC) in computing your income in the year. In future years, the full amount of annuity payments received under the IAAC will be included in your income in the year of receipt. Therefore, the overall effect of purchasing an IAAC is to distribute the tax cost associated with the eligible income receipt over any number of years you may choose, including a life annuity; however, the guaranteed term cannot go beyond age eighty-five.

If you have eligible income in [1980] and wish to purchase an IAAC, you must do it before February 29, [1981]. Should you borrow the funds to make the IAAC purchase, the interest on such borrowings will be deductible.

Savings through Income Reductions

Capital transactions

The decision to sell securities should be based upon good investment reasoning and not on tax considerations. However, if you are holding loss investments which you intend to sell in the near future, you might consider taking advantage of a procedure commonly referred to as "tax-loss selling". Within limits, one-half of the loss you realize on selling such a "loser" (the allowable capital loss) is deductible in computing your income for the year. To the extent that you have taxable capital gains realized in the year, you may deduct allowable capital losses sufficient to offset those gains. In addition, you may deduct an additional $2,000 of your allowable capital losses against other income (i.e. professional, employment, investment, or other income). In so doing, you are able to reduce the cost of your "loser" by using the loss to protect other income from tax.

To the extent that you are not fully able to utilize your allowable capital loss in the current year, you can carry the excess back one year and forward indefinitely to be deducted in those years in the same manner that they were

161

deductible in the current year. This also provides some room for tax planning. If you intend to dispose of various assets, some of which will give rise to large taxable capital gains (eligible income for an IAAC) and some to large allowable capital losses, you may effectively defer the taxes on other income by properly timing the dispositions and concurrently buying an IAAC. For instance, if you realize the capital gains this year and use the proceeds to buy an IAAC, then in [1981] you sell the loss assets, you can carry the loss realized in [1981] back to [1980] to offset the taxable capital gains realized in [1980.] This does not disqualify the tax deductibility of the IAAC and effectively allows you to use the IAAC to defer tax on other income which is not eligible for the purchase of an IAAC. The theory also works in reverse by realizing the losses in [1980] and the gains in [1981] concurrently with the purchase of an IAAC in [1981]. This reversal also has the added benefit in that you do not have to purchase the IAAC until February [1982.]

In taking advantage of any of these particular procedures you should be careful to ensure that you do not fall into the trap of "superficial losses". If you realize a capital loss from the disposition of an asset where the same or an identical asset is acquired by yourself or your spouse or certain other related parties during the period from thirty days after the disposition of the loss property, you will not be allowed to deduct that capital loss.

You should also be aware that to ensure the recognition of security transactions in [1980], the settlement date must occur before December 31, [1980.] Therefore, you should make all such transactions before December 20, [1980] as it normally requires five business days to complete a trading transaction (from date of sale to settlement date).

Business investment losses

If you own shares or debt of a Canadian controlled private corporation (CCPC) which, in effect, are worthless because the company has been unsuccessful, you may now receive more favourable treatment on the disposition of those securities than that which is applied to the disposition of other capital investments. If the CCPC has gone bankrupt in the year or if you dispose of the securities in the year in an arm's length transaction, you will realize a "business investment loss" on the disposition of your shares or debt. One-half of the business investment loss (the allowable business investment loss) is fully deductible from income from all sources in the year. To the extent that it cannot be fully utilized in the year, the excess can be carried back one year and forward five years and may be deductible in those years on the same basis as it was in the current year. You should note, however, that a proposal in the November 16, 1978 Federal Budget, which was reintroduced in Parliament in Bill C-17 on October 25, 1979, will reduce the business investment loss realized on a share which was issued before 1972 (or on a share substituted or exchanged for that original share) by the amount of any taxable dividends in respect of that share received by the shareholder or a related person, since 1971.

Deductibility of interest costs

If you have some personal savings, but not sufficient to cover all your personal and investment expenditure needs, and therefore, must borrow some funds to cover the excess, you should consider borrowing to purchase your investment rather than for your personal needs. The interest costs on money borrowed to earn income is tax deductible.

Generally, interest costs will be tax deductible on money borrowed for the following purposes:

- to make past service contributions to a registered pension fund;
- to make a contribution to an RRSP for yourself (but not for your spouse);
- to purchase an IAAC;
- to purchase investments which will produce taxable income;
- for general business purposes.

Therefore, it is obviously preferable, if you have a choice, to use borrowed funds for one of the purposes suggested above rather than to purchase the family car or the family cottage. In addition, where you have a further choice, it is preferable to use borrowed funds to purchase investments not eligible for the investment income deduction [of up to $1,000] or to make contributions to your RRSP rather than to purchase investments which will be eligible for the investment income deduction. Interest costs on these eligible investments will reduce the investment income deduction.

If you have outstanding debts on which the interest is not deductible, and at the same time you have funds available to make a contribution to a deferred income plan or to purchase investments, you might consider using your own funds to repay the existing loans and then make fresh borrowings for your contribution to your plan for your purchase of income-producing assets.

Charitable donations

To be deductible in [1980], you must make your charitable donations by December 31, [1980]. Your overall limitation on deductions in the year is 20% of your net income for the year. To the extent that your donations exceed this limit, you are permitted to carry them forward and use them next year (subject to the same limitation).

Donations which qualify as gifts to the Crown or as gifts of cultural property under the Cultural Property Export and Import Act are not subject to the 20% limitation for charitable donations. In addition, further preferential tax treatment is accorded to property gifted under the Cultural Property Export and Import Act.

Medical expenses

To the extent that your qualifying medical expenses incurred in the year exceed 3% of your income for the year, you may deduct the excess in computing your taxable income. The qualifying medical expenses used in the calculation may be for any twelve month period ending in the year as long as none of those expenses were included in the previous year's deduction. Therefore, if you have substantial expenses this year which may continue into next year, and you were not able to utilize those expenses in 1979 because they did not exceed 3% of your income, the receipts should be saved because you may be able to use them in the calculation of qualifying medical expenses for 1980.

Political contributions

If you contribute to a registered federal political party or a candidate in a federal by-election in [1980,] before December 31, you will be eligible for the federal tax credit for political contributions in [1980.] The maximum credit is $500 for qualified contributions of $1,150.

If you make contributions to registered provincial parties in Ontario or constituent associations and election candidates for the provincial parliament, you will be eligible for the Ontario tax credit for individuals which is similar to the federal tax credit.

Postage Stamps and Coins: For the Collector

Stamps

Perhaps surprisingly one of the best inflation hedges has proven to be old stamps. The total value of every unused U.S. postage stamp between 1882 to 1909 rose from $4,444 in 1954 to $39,389 in 1977. This is a rise of 786% which far outperformed the stock market (and even gold) during that period. The boom in stamps shows no sign of slowing down, for the 1979 Scott Catalogue shows an average 20% rise in the price of classic U.S. stamps from 1978. Airmail stamps from before the war have done even better. Here are some examples of typical investment-quality stamps from Scott catalogues.

Description (Unused Stamps) and Catalogue Number	1959	1980	Average % Increase in Value Per Annum*
CANADA	$	$	%
1924, 2¢ green, Cat. no. 137	5.00	52.50	45.24
1937, 2¢ brown, Cat. no. 232	.08	.60	30.95
1953, $1 gray, Cat. no. 321	2.00	25.00	54.76
UNITED STATES			
1924, 5¢ dark blue, Cat. no. 616	6.00	45.00	30.95
1932, 6¢ red orange, Cat. no. 711	.65	5.00	31.87
1956, $5 black, Cat. no. 1053	10.00	125.00	54.76

U.S. Stamps

According to Scott, the next table lists *all* "regular stamps issued by the United States Government and listed consecutively in Scott's Catalogue between 1901 and 1938 *without exception*; that is to say, a total of 541 different stamps. Average percentage increase in value per year over more than twenty years of these stamps was 39.78%. This is similar to taking in alphabetical order 541 stocks which were listed consecutively on the New York Stock Exchange in 1959 and comparing them with their value in 1980 including those companies which, in the meantime, have disappeared."

* Calculated as a percentage of original catalogue value.

Years of Issue and Catalogue Nos.	1959	1980	Average % Increase in Value Per Annum*
	$	$	%
1901 to 1903 Cat. no. 294-319	423.30	4,734.50	48.50
1906 to 1909 Cat. no. 320-373	1,354.80	9,178.50	27.50
1910 to 1913 Cat. no. 374-396	102.65	1,006.75	41.94
1914 to 1938 Cat. no. 397-834	1,906.15	20,500.14	46.45
			39.78%

Prices for Canadian Stamps

Canadian stamps have proven even more profitable than American, as illustrated by the following table. Listings are given for all "regular stamps issued by the Canadian Government between 1851 and 1946 *without exception*; that is to say, a total of 273 stamps. Average percentage increase in value per year over more than twenty years was 40.64%." according to Scott.

Years of Issue and Catalogue Nos.	1959	1980	Average % Increase in Value Per Annum*
	$	$	%
1851 to 1897 Cat. no. 1-73	4,139.25	36,831.50	37.61
1898 to 1899 Cat. no. 74-88	51.62	729.00	62.49
1903 to 1912 Cat. no. 89-122	126.53	2,007.00	70.77
1912 to 1946 Cat. no. 123-273	154.53	3,068.85	89.81
			40.64%

* Calculated as a percentage of original catalogue value.

The reason for this tremendous boom is purely and simply inflation. Investors are seeking out things that will hold their value as the dollar sinks. There are far more people buying postage stamps than any other collectable simply because tens of thousands of adults learned their expertise from their childhood hobby. It is also far easier to invest in stamps where everything is catalogued than in old snuff boxes where every item has a different value.

There are a few basic rules:

(1) Specialize. It is hard enough to learn about the stamps from one country without attempting to cover the world. It is always best to collect the stamps from your own nation.

(2) Buy only old stamps, the older the better. There is no profit to be made in collecting modern commemoratives which are turned out by the million.

(3) Buy only perfect copies. Damaged stamps will sell for a tiny fraction of the catalogue price and are extremely slow to rise in price.

(4) Mint stamps go up in price faster than used ones. But if you are buying mint copies buy ones that have not been hinged.

(5) Avoid the stamps of defunct countries because they tend to have too few collectors to produce a wide market.

(6) Do patronize the auction houses. Their prices tend to be lower than dealers' prices.

Many persons who do not have the confidence or the knowledge to buy stamps for themselves are now investing in them through stamp investment firms like Amberley Investment. These companies have made a great deal of money in the last five years by selling stamp packages in amounts ranging from $500 to $250,000 to investors who leave the choice of the stamps up to the investment company. All such companies offer to repurchase their stamps at any time at the current market price. Because of the inflation boom, all of their clients have made money so far. Amberley boasts that:

> Clients who held them for more than 24 months always made a substantial gain. The average gain for clients who resold their stamp shipments back to us after 24 to 36 months was 63%, with the lowest gain being 35.28% and the highest gain 90.91%.
>
> Clients who held them for more than 3 years have in no case made less than a 70% gain. The average gain of clients in cases of such repurchases was 88%. The highest gain was 106%.

An investor will do better investing on his own provided he has the required knowledge about these little bits of paper. Obviously all the investment companies in this business are there to make money for themselves. If, however, an investor has no expertise an investment company offers a reasonable alternative.

Stamps vs. Purchasing Power of the Dollar*

From January 1969 to December 1977, the purchasing power of the dollar declined by more than 40%. Prices of selected fine stamps showed an average annual increase in value of over 20%, thus an increase of over 200% during this period.

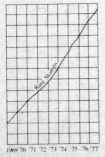

Reprinted with permission from Amberley Investment.

Coins

In recent years, coin collecting has boomed, but just as in the stamp field, one must be discriminating. I have already discussed collecting coins for their gold content, but outside of gold coins it is plain foolish to collect any modern coinage. It just isn't possible for any scarcity value to develop and the metal value of today's coins is only a fraction of their face value. This leaves for consideration old coins from the United States or Canada or ancient coins. While it is true that in recent years prices in this area have gone up by about 15% annually, these coins are neither easy to value or to sell at anywhere near retail price. Price depends upon both scarcity and condition but this hobby is now plagued by forgeries the better of which are almost impossible to distinguish from the real thing. *Unless you are a real expert, I would warn investors away from old coins.*

There is one relatively safe way the amateur can invest in old coins. Bowers & Ruddy Galleries*, a subsidiary of General Mills, have set up a collector's investment program. The investor deposits $100 per month or more and receives in return diversified collections of U.S. coins of various dates, sizes and series. There is no guarantee as to how well they will do in the future but their past record is impressive, showing an average gain of 20% per year since 1974. This is not my first choice as an inflation hedge, but if collecting coins turns you on this is an easy way to begin.

And in times of rapid inflation coin investing certainly can be very lucrative. Edward Lee of Lee Numismatics reported in the December 10, 1979 issue of *Barron's* that

High quality rare coins have appreciated by 70% at the wholesale level in just twelve months. My statistics are

*6922 Hollywood Boulevard, Los Angeles.

172

based on ninety different types of uncirculated United States coins and thirty-three types of proof coins. These coins cover every major denomination from the late 18th century to the era of World War II. Literally thousands of coins are included....

The range of increases was quite wide with some copper coins appreciating by "only" 12% and proof dollars up by more than 300%. This wide range of prices clearly points out the need for professional advice. On the other hand any form of investment that appreciates by 12% at the worst, clearly demands careful investigation....

This enviable record of high profitability combined with extremely low downside risk answers the 'why' of the exceptional interest in numismatic investments.

Memorabilia and the Greater Fool Theory

During those Halycon days back in the fifties when stock promoters sold millions of dollars worth of worthless stock to gullible investors, the buyers were always told that the stock was going much higher and that they would be able to sell out at double or triple their cost. Most of them bought in the naive belief that at a later date there would be another sucker prepared to pay even higher prices for their vastly overvalued certificates — this was the greater fool theory.

Today the greater fool theory is shown in the lust for memorabilia.

Inflation is invariably accompanied by fiscal madnesses in investments, as well as in paper money, and memorabilia is a perfect example. Memorabilia is nostalgia, things that have no real value but remind people of their youth. Articles of memorabilia invariably become sought after when paper money loses its value. Thus old comic books can sell for thousands of dollars, a Mickey Mouse watch can bring $250, and an Elvis Presley doll recently sold for $1,000. The same phenomenon took place during the great German inflation with General Ludendorf dolls selling for thousands of marks, but just fifteen years later the price of Germany's memorabilia from the Kaiser's time totally collapsed never to recover. The reason is simple enough. Memorabilia holds its value only so long as collectors from that era retain their nostalgia. As that generation of collectors begins to die off, so does the demand for the junk of their youth.

I cannot advise my readers strongly enough — *memorabilia is a foolish place to put money*. Even depreciating cash is a better speculation than old baseball cards, toys, beer cans, or coca cola signs.

Limited Editions

Limited editions are just as bad and it seems as though every current magazine carries an ad for a new limited edition of something. The sad fact is that although a lot of money has been made from limited editions it has almost all gone into the pockets of the manufacturers of this new craze. The Franklin Mint began the whole thing and they now have a lot of imitators, who produce objects designed to appeal to the desire for real things during an inflation. The problem with these real things is that they are sold far above their actual value and, because they are being continually poured into the market, no true scarcity can develop. A recent survey showed that most purchases from these mints cannot be resold at cost let alone show a profit.

The appeal made to investors in ads for limited editions is quite clever. Here is a pitch from an issue of *Money Magazine*:

The special attraction of collector's plates is that they are original, limited-edition works of art as well as a measurable investment with a well-established secondary market. The most prized editions have outperformed even the most glamorous securities.

Plate collecting possesses many unique advantages not found in other forms of art collecting and investments. Unlike stamps and coins, collector's plates are original works of art issued in limited edition. They are meant to be displayed and appreciated while stamps and coins are hidden away in albums. Most importantly, no stamp or coin is usually issued as a limited edition while every collector's plate is.

A comparison with antiques is misleading. Even the oldest collector's plates aren't antiques by the generally accepted definition. And the fast-moving market in plates hardly compares with the slow, involved trading of antiques.

These appeals are amazingly successful. According to the same ad there were 2.2 million collectors of these plates in the United States as of the end of 1977 and they estimate that figure will double this year.

And all of this proves that Barnum was right!

Photographs

Collecting old photos is being aggressively promoted by a few galleries, but if ever there was a bubble about to burst, this is it. Any photograph can be reproduced by a clever technician with or without a negative in unlimited amounts. This area is not for intelligent investors.

Autographs

This is an interesting hobby but hardly the place to put serious money. The market is too thin and dealers markups are far too high.

Dolls

Same situation. Okay as a hobby; lousy as an investment.

Books

A very important and booming field, but too much specialized knowledge is required. The amateur should leave this one to professionals.

Rugs

Too late. Prices have already gone to dizzy and, in my opinion, unrealistic levels.

Three Plans to Follow

Even for those who understand inflation the route to financial success is not obvious, because there are so many possible roads to follow. This book has talked about gold and antiques, stamps and coins, real estate and GNMAs, but where and how should one start and what proportion of money should go into each type of investment? That key question must be answered differently depending on the investor's age, resources, and responsibilities. Therefore, the first edition of this book laid out three different options for my readers. For most people there was no salvation from the forthcoming financial disaster simply because they had nothing with which to work. Every time I appear on an open line show the first question I receive is invariably "What should someone do who has nothing to invest?" I can only reply, "With nothing, you can do nothing except pray for a miracle." The terrible truth is that the vast majority of people in Canada and the United States fall into this category. However, it is unlikely that many of them read this book.

Who are my readers? Coneducor, a company for which I write and that has sold tens of thousands of courses in investing in the United States and Canada, did a survey and determined that a typical subscriber was male, age 42, married with two children. His annual income ranges from $15,000 to $30,000 and his net worth is $125,000 to $150,000 consisting mainly of an equity in a personal residence, plus $10,000 to $15,000 in a locked-in pension plan, plus about $10,000 to $20,000 in other investments. His annual savings consists of $3,000 to $4,000 in cash, plus a gradual increase in equity in his home. His occupation is middle management in a larger corporation or he is a professional such as a doctor, dentist or engineer (but he is not an accountant), or the owner of a small independent business. His I.Q. tends to be higher than the average and he tends to be relatively sophisticated about finance.

This investor has the most to lose from inflation, for it is this category that has suffered the worst from previous inflations, and yet this is the investor who has the resources to protect himself by using his equity more wisely. For him, I suggested Plan One.

Plan One

You own a home purchased ten years ago for $75,000 which now is worth $160,000 and on which there is still a $35,000 mortgage. You have $12,000 in a pension plan which you can't touch and you own $15,000 in government bonds and blue chip stocks. In addition, you have about $10,000 in equity in whole life insurance and you have $2,000 or $3,000 tied up in a hobby — stamps or coins, antiques, jewellery or oriental rugs, or dolls. In whatever field it is, presumably it is one in which you have developed some expertise. This is what you should do:

(1) Purchase enough term insurance to cover your family's needs for the next five years and then cash in your whole life insurance. Don't cash in the insurance first, just in case you are no longer insurable.

(2) If your pension plan is cashable, cash it in even if this requires paying an immediate tax.

(3) Sell your government bonds and blue chip stocks.

(4) Renegotiate your mortgage, increasing it to the *maximum* on which you can afford to meet the payments from your *current* income.

After the previous manoeuvres have been completed, you should have approximately $100,000 in cash. I would invest this as follows:

(1) $5,000 in Krugerrand which should be kept in a safety deposit vault.

(2) $15,000 divided between wealth in the ground stocks like Dome Mines, Campbell Red Lake, Homestake, Denison, International Nickel, Pacific Pete, Hudsons Bay Oil & Gas or Imperial Oil, with most of it going into the first three.

(3) $55,000 into gold bullion.

(4) $20,000 into your hobby, be it stamps, coins or whatever, provided:
    (a) your hobby is not a fad — such as photography or memorabilia.
    (b) you know that you have the knowledge and experience,
    (c) there is an international market for your purchases,
    (d) you buy only the best pieces.

(5) The last $5,000 should be used in an attempt to grab the brass ring. The average American and Canadian moron tries to do this by buying lottery tickets. You will have much better odds for your money, if you put this $5,000 into the currency or commodity markets, buying gold, Swiss francs, or German marks. You may lose your $5,000 but you just might walk away with a million.

Plan Two

My second largest category of readers is the widow class. She is fifty to sixty years old and has been left an estate of $175,000 by her husband, most of which was in the form of insurance plus an equity in a house, and she has had little or no financial experience. By the time she seeks my advice, she has sold the home and has invested the entire sum in government bonds. I am often consulted by such ladies but they rarely, if ever, follow my advice because "I need the money invested to give me an income".

It is very difficult to get this type of person to change their thinking of a lifetime, which demands that they seek "security". It is very hard to explain that government bonds are not "security". It's tragic but these people will lose their entire stake during inflation, all the while clinging to the dual myths of security and yield. If any of you were in this category and were willing to listen, I suggested you follow Plan Two:

(1) Forget about security and yield for they no longer exist. Keep enough cash or government bonds to pay for your running expenses for the next year and divide the remaining $160,000 as follows.

(2) Buy a bungalow in the suburbs. In most areas this is

still possible for $75,000. If you can stand it mentally, mortgage it, but if this is too painful, pay for it outright.

(3) Put all the rest of your money into gold, divided as follows: 10% in Krugerrand, 60% in bullion, and the balance in one of the top U.S. or Canadian gold stocks.

(4) When your cash runs out and you need money for living expenses, sell your gold but only as you need it. This way your money will last much longer than it will in its current situation.

Plan Three

My third category of reader is young, in his early twenties, bright, ambitious, just starting out in his career with just a few thousand dollars to work with. To this person I recommended Plan Three:

Take a chance. You may lose your stake and have to start again but this is the one time in your life when you will be able to take that chance. I was in this category 25 years ago and I took a chance with my stake and won. As a result I have lived like a prince ever since. If you lose you won't be that far behind where you are now, but if you win your whole future will be changed. I think the best chance today is in the futures market. With $2,500 you can purchase one hundred ounces of gold for delivery in one year at a price of $235. You might lose the $2,500 but with a little luck you may make many times that amount.

Looking back over the past year I am delighted at how well that advice has worked out. Those persons who followed plan one have doubled their money, the widows in plan two have seen their assets go up by at least a third, while the young speculators who followed plan three have made literal fortunes. *The $2,500 invested last year is worth at least $30,000* today and if pyramiding was used has grown to over a million dollars!

And it wasn't all just theory. I have received hundreds of letters from people who followed my advice and made oodles of money. Today the numbers are different but the situation is still the same. Inflation will continue to accelerate. Politicians will continue to print paper money. Gold, real estate and all real things will continue to rise in value. Canada Savings Bonds, bank deposits and mortgages will continue to shrink in terms of buying power. *Plans one, two and three are still valid today.*

Why Are There so Many Books on Investing?

Every year, dozens of new books come out, each giving a different formula on how to get rich. They all seem to do well — at least for their authors and publishers. But I think the public must get very confused. Who is to be believed?

In the 1960s, a dance instructor named Nicholas Darvas wrote his story of *How I made Two Million Dollars in the Stock Market*.[1] Buyers of the book discovered that the author's chief tool was to put in orders to sell stocks if they went down and to hold his winners that were going up. But those who tried to follow Darvas' method lost money as the market whipsawed.

Ten years later, Harry Browne in his *How to Profit from a Monetary Crisis*[2] advised the purchase of gold, Swiss francs, a house in the country, a supply of canned goods, and a gun to fight off the neighbours once the rioting began. Poor Harry's timing couldn't have been worse. There have been no riots and his recommended gold purchase

[1] New York: American Research Council, 1960.
[2] Toronto: McGraw-Hill, 1974. New York: Macmillan, 1974.

came just as gold ownership became legal in the U.S. and the metal's price plummeted. Harry Browne profited from his experience and in his 1978 book, *New Profits from the Monetary Crisis*,[3] was not so certain about the future, suggesting that gold and foreign currencies might go in either direction.

That same year Andrew Tobias in *The Only Investment Guide You'll Ever Need*[4] warned against buying "antique cars, wine, autographs, stamps, coins, diamonds, art" for two reasons: (1) You are competing against experts. (2) These things don't pay dividends and are hard for an amateur to sell because there is such a spread between retail and wholesale.

In 1978 there was even a college professor, Don Abrams, who published a book on stock market advice, called *The Profit Takers*,[5] in which his entire strategy consisted of buying convertible bonds and simultaneously selling short stock in the same company, a plan certain to enrich brokers if not investors. The author calmly assured his readers that his technique would "pluck profits from the stock market no matter how it moves — up or down". Alas, as investors who tried the system discovered, it was no panacea.

All through 1979, Howard Ruff's *How to Prosper During the Coming Bad Years* (Times Books, 1979) was on the best-seller list with its prescription to buy dehydrated foods and to hoard bags of silver dollars. I tried the dried foods and the taste was so bad I decided we'd do better to suffer the inflation and the riots Mr. Ruff predicts.

The sad fact is that most investment books are written not by millionaires who have made money in the market, but by authors who hope to make money with their advice.

[3]New York: Morrow, 1978.
[4]New York: Harcourt, Brace, Jovanovich, 1978.
[5]New York: Deneau & Greenberg, 1978.

And as a result much of the material in these books, no matter how well meant, is misleading or just bad advice.

The other important factor is that times are changing very rapidly. A book written just two years ago may already be out of date while one written five years ago is entirely useless. I reread my own best seller *Anyone Can Make a Million* recently and was shocked at how dated the advice has become. Even the second edition of this book will eventually suffer the same fate.

In addition, no one can be right all the time. I'm proud of the recommendations in my books which have been very close to the mark, but I am not immune from blunders. I have made two classic mistakes. In 1966, I recommended the purchase of convertible bonds, which up to then had been the perfect investment. This was followed by the simultaneous collapse of both the stock and bond markets and with them all too many convertible bonds. More recently in 1971, I advised the purchase of wine for investment following the magnificent Bordeaux vintages of 1970 and 1971. My recommendation was followed by the three horrible years of 1972, 1973 and 1974 which produced barely drinkable, let alone profitable, wine.

I had intended to make a list here of all the investment books on the market with a summation of their bad advice, but my publisher became discouraged by my first venture in the field. I did a somewhat unkind review of a new book on stock advice and challenged the author to give four specific suggestions for investments. When three of these went bust, I wrote it up in my *Toronto Sun* column and the author responded with a million dollar lawsuit. He finally did offer to settle, if I'd pay his legal expenses of $2,000. I declined his kind offer.

Another problem is that even when investment advice is correct, it may break down if too many people follow it.

Thus in *Anyone Can Make A Million*, I recommended free riding, the purchase and sale of bonds and stocks without paying for them. My advice was received far too well. When thousands of investors began to practice what only a handful had done up to then, the regulating authorities passed laws eliminating free riding. Similarly in the same book, I advised the purchase of Supertest stock at $18. It really was undervalued at that price but not many people were able to profit from it. As my readers rushed to buy, the stock quickly moved up to $40 where it was bought out by another firm.

There is no simple road to riches. Investors want to be given uncomplicated rules that will make them rich. But there are no such firm rules because the game and its rules are constantly changing. If Harry Browne had brought his first book out four years earlier, or three years later, he would have been spectacularly correct. It was not his advice that was bad; it was his timing.

My timing in last year's edition of this book was extraordinarily fortunate, for literally everything I recommended has soared upwards. Obviously I can't tell now how well my timing will be with the second edition, but in one way this book is different from all others. Of course it contains rules and recommendations, but they are secondary to the message I'm trying to impart. *Inflation is here — it's not going away. Get rid of paper investments. Buy equity.* My timing may be good or bad but I know that five years down the road, no one following this advice will regret it.

It really isn't deciding whom to believe. It's a matter of examining the economic facts in the United States and Canada. If you have come to the same conclusions that I have, this book will give you some solid indication of how to protect yourself and profit during inflation.

MERCHANTS OF GRAIN

Dan Morgan

Dan Morgan is the first journalist ever to penetrate the secrecy that surrounds the oligopoly of grain. In *Merchants of Grain* he reveals how the five privately owned giants of the grain industry conduct their intricate, dramatic and secretive business of buying and selling food all over the world. Somehow, until now, these multinational corporations have managed to slip through history inconspicuously, despite the fact that they are, not only powerful enough to control the pricing and marketing of all Canadian grain, but could ultimately influence the direction of international politics.

"One of the most informative and interesting non-fiction works of the decade." — *Hamilton Spectator*

"A pioneering book that illuminates a shadowy part of international economy." — *Ottawa Citizen*

"It is simply an awesome book." — *Regina Leader-Post*

OIL AND WORLD POWER (Fifth Edition)

Peter R. Odell

International issues from Rhodesia to Sino-Soviet relations are influenced by considerations of oil production and consumption. The international communications network of the larger oil companies rivals that of the majority of nations. In 1950 the world's crude oil production was only 500 million tons. By 1977 it had risen to over 3,000 million and may double in size again by the end of the century. This completely revised and expanded fifth edition presents and evaluates the traumatic events in the oil empire since 1973. The changes in the power structure which have resulted are fundamental and have immense implications for future economic and political developments.

THE PENGUIN DICTIONARY OF COMPUTERS
(Second Edition)

*Anthony Chandor with John Graham
and Robin Williamson*

The Penguin Dictionary of Computers has been designed
to assist both technical readers and the increasing number of non-specialists whose work is to some extent
affected by a computer. Exactly what computer techni-
cians are referring to when they speak of 'critical path
methods', 'modular programming', 'truth tables' or
'crippled leap-frog tests' is clearly and concisely ex-
plained in an alphabetical list of definitions with cross-
references.

The entries are interspersed with seventy general articles which cover, more fully, the major computer topics
and such business processes as 'budgetary control' and
'systems analysis'.

THE PENGUIN DICTIONARY OF ECONOMICS
(Second Edition)

*Graham Bannock, R. E. Baxter
and Ray Rees*

The Penguin Dictionary of Economics is addressed to
both the student and the general reader who wants to
be able to follow economic discussions in the press and
elsewhere, or whose daily work demands some familiar-
ity with economic terms. Prepared by three practising
economists, it contains over 1,600 entries, and includes
discussion of the history of economics and individual
economists who have made a definable contribution to
contemporary economic thought. An elaborate system
of cross-referencing makes this dictionary easy to use
and extremely informative.